The Yale Library of N

Donald Kagan and Frederick

CROSSING THE LINE

A BLUEJACKET'S ODYSSEY IN WORLD WAR II

ALVIN KERNAN

Foreword by DONALD KAGAN and FREDERICK KAGAN

Introduction by LAWRENCE STONE

Yale University Press / New Haven and London

First Yale University Press edition, 2007.
First published by Naval Institute Press in 1994.

Designed by Mary Valencia.
Set in Minion by Tseng Information Systems, Inc., Durham, North Carolina.
Printed in the United States of America.

Library of Congress Cataloging-in-Publication Data
Kernan, Alvin B.
Crossing the line : a Bluejacket's odyssey in World War II /
Alvin Kernan ; foreword by Donald Kagan and Frederick Kagan ;
introduction by Lawrence Stone. — 1st Yale University Press ed.
p. cm. — (The Yale library of military history)
Originally published: Annapolis : Naval Institute Press, 1994.
Includes index.
ISBN: 978-0-300-12315-9 (alk. paper)
1. Kernan, Alvin B. 2. World War, 1939–1945—Naval operations,
American. 3. World War, 1939–1945—Campaigns—Pacific Ocean.
4. World War, 1939–1945—Personal narratives, American.
5. Sailors—United States—Biography. I. Title.
D773.K46 2007
940.54′5973092—dc22
[B]
2006038455

A catalogue record for this book is available from the British Library.

The paper in this book meets the guidelines for permanence and
durability of the Committee on Production Guidelines for
Book Longevity of the Council on Library Resources.

10 9 8 7 6 5 4 3 2 1

For my children

CONTENTS

FOREWORD

War has been a subject of intense interest from the beginning of literature around the world. Whether it be in the earliest literary work in the Western tradition, Homer's *Iliad*, or the Rigvedic hymns of ancient India, people have always been fascinated by this dangerous and challenging phenomenon. Few can fail to be stirred by such questions as: How and why do wars come about? How and why do they end? Why did the winners win and the losers lose? How do leaders make life-and-death decisions? Why do combatants follow orders that put their lives at risk? How do individuals and societies behave in war, and how are they affected by it? Recent events have raised the study of war from one of intellectual interest to a matter of vital importance to Americans and the world. Ordinary citizens must understand war in order to choose their leaders wisely, and leaders must understand it if they are to prevent wars where possible and win them when necessary.

This series, therefore, seeks to present the keenest analyses of war in its different aspects, the sharpest evaluations of political and military decision-making, and descriptive accounts of military activity that illuminate its human elements. It will do so drawing on the full range of military history from ancient times to the present and in every part of the globe in order to make available to the general public readable and accurate scholarly accounts of this most fascinating and dangerous of human activities.

Alvin Kernan, the author of *The Unknown Battle of Midway,* is a teacher and scholar of great experience and outstanding talent who has made a great name for himself in both fields at Yale and Princeton. But on

December 8, 1941, he was a seaman on the USS *Enterprise* as she made her way among the burning hulks of the American Pacific Fleet to a berth at Pearl Harbor. *Crossing the Line* is the gripping story of his personal experience of the rest of World War II in the Pacific. In vivid yet economical prose, Kernan describes the Battle of Midway, the sinking of the USS *Hornet,* air combat over Guadalcanal, and many other critical battles in which he had a hand.

As the story of a young man's experience of war, *Crossing the Line* is penetrating and circumspect. Kernan's historical study of the events he lived through gives real context to his own memories. The lively interplay between his recollections and subsequent examinations makes this an unusual face-of-battle account. Kernan does not ask the reader to believe what he says just because he was there. He uses his participation in events, instead, to offer new insights within the context of solid research.

Crossing the Line is an important book for the insight it offers into the war at sea of the Greatest Generation, into the nature of naval combat from an unusual perspective, and for the lessons it offers about how young men react to their experiences of war.

It is also the personal story of the price America paid for its military unpreparedness before World War II. As Kernan argued in *The Unknown Battle of Midway,* the first book in this series, the American peacetime navy was profoundly unready for war. In *Crossing the Line* anecdotes sometimes reminiscent of *The Caine Mutiny* illustrate the slowness and inadequacy of the navy's response to the outbreak of the war. Military organizations are shaped in peacetime but forged in war, and the price of that forging is paid in lives. *Crossing the Line* offers many a cautionary tale for a nation at war.

Donald Kagan and Frederick Kagan

INTRODUCTION

My qualifications for writing an introduction to Alvin Kernan's frank, vivid, and moving description of his experiences in the navy during World War II are as follows. After serving in several ships from a destroyer to a battleship, I too ended up, like Kernan, in an escort carrier in the western Pacific off Japan. We were both part of the Seventh Fleet, which was the greatest battle fleet ever assembled, under the command of Admiral Nimitz, and the most amazingly efficient organization I have ever seen in my life. My aircraft carrier, HMS *Chaser,* had been sent to serve in the Pacific, partly to help the Americans but mostly to make sure that, in a fit of anticolonial enthusiasm, they did not give Hong Kong back to the Chinese at the end of the war. In this we were successful, being the first ship to enter the harbor after the Japanese surrender.

Kernan and I joined our respective navies from noticeably different backgrounds. He was abruptly wrenched out of civilian life on a remote, isolated ranch in Wyoming and thrown into the traumatic experience of boot camp. I was similarly wrenched out of civilian life, but in my case this meant cozy rooms, good food, and a servant to wait on me, all of which were provided to prewar students at Oxford University. After boot camp at Shotley and nine months on the lower deck of HMS *Fuji,* I was sent back home for officer training and thereafter served in the comfortable, if alcoholic, atmosphere of a British naval officers' wardroom.

Kernan saw much action, exhibited great bravery, and was many times very nearly killed; once he even had to abandon his sinking ship. Although I was involved in several dangerous operations, including two convoys to Malta and two to Murmansk, my life was in imminent danger only once. Kernan served as a gunner on a plane, frequently in fierce combat, while

I sat in a windowless office as senior aircraft controller, directing planes like his to their missions. But as I read his story, again and again I find myself thinking, yes, this is exactly how it was.

The author encapsulates the culture and ideology of the U.S. Navy of that time in a series of shrewd observations. For example, "Cleanliness was not next to godliness in the United States Navy; it was godliness." Boot camp, with its endless drill on the "grinder," was designed to force you "to put your individuality in storage. . . . Reasonable excuses were not part of this life." For me, on the other hand, the benefits of low cunning were also part of boot camp. I soon made an arrangement with the chief petty officer by which I would take charge of our squad after 1600, leaving him free to go home. In exchange, he left me alone all day—time which I spent reading Proust in the laundry (the only place where I could be both warm and safe from discovery). The culture of the U.S. Navy as described by Kernan is identical with that to be found in the British navy of the same period. More remarkable is the similar inefficiency of our navies' planes and, especially, the torpedoes with which both fleets were provided in the early stages of the war. (When I complained to a senior officer, he retorted that British torpedoes were excellent in peacetime— that is, on maneuvers—since they could be relied upon to come to the surface after firing and so to be used again!) Only the Japanese and the Germans seem to have been able to manufacture effective torpedoes. In the end, victory came from the sheer volume of military hardware, plus advanced radar, success in decoding, and, as at the Battle of Midway, to which Kernan devotes a riveting chapter, a lot of luck.

Kernan notes the brutality of life as a seaman during wartime, a life he describes as "healthy but in many respects like a chain gang." He reminds us that in times of crisis all hands were on four-hour shifts (four on, four off) throughout the day and night, so that one was perpetually tired. He also remembers the torments of heat rash in the tropics. Nor does he ever forget that "death lived on an aircraft carrier operating in wartime conditions." One day a plane would crash on takeoff; the next day a plane would crash on landing. And it was all too easy for one of the flight deck crew to take a false step and get chewed up by a propeller.

Sometimes "planes went out on patrol and were never heard of again." This was particular agony to me, as I called the plane for hours on the radio and listened as the signals became fainter and fainter, ending in a total silence. Kernan rightly lays great stress on the sheer boredom of life during the long stretches between the brief moments of sheer terror. He describes how the Americans spent their time playing cards for money, often all day long. It was mostly poker, and the gambling was for high stakes. The British did the same, but the stakes were very much lower. We could never have pulled off Kernan's last financial coup. We tended to play liar's dice, the loser buying drinks all round, and for a while we played endless games of Monopoly. The conversation, such as it was, was mostly about sex and girls, if only because they were in such short supply.

The author deals discreetly but frankly with the sexual problems and temptations for young sailors on periods of leave. Prostitutes were readily available in every naval base, but they were not always free from venereal disease. I do not know what happened in the Pacific theater, since our rear base was Sydney, Australia, but in the Mediterranean theater—in Algiers, Naples, Rome, etc.—the U.S. Army tried to deal with this problem by organizing medically supervised brothels, some for officers and others for enlisted men, as so vividly described in Joseph Heller's Catch 22. A young man has to lose his virginity sometime, and Kernan observes that "sex and war really initiate us into society," while the former provides some intense pleasure "in a world that offers a lot of dullness and pain."

But Kernan does not fail to mention the good times and the nobler aspects of a sailor's life in wartime. For example, "the instant love affair" with whatever ship one happened to be assigned to. He observes, correctly, that "to a young man war is exciting." At that age—eighteen, nineteen, twenty—we all thought that we were immortal. It was only the older men, worried about a wife and children, who were constantly afraid of death. There was no great hostility toward the Japanese, who, rightly, "were regarded as a worthy foe." Taken all in all, "we saw the war as a natural and rare chance to live life at least close to something great." The Seventh Fleet off Japan was one of the most amazing sights we would ever behold—a gigantic armada spread out over miles and miles of ocean, the vast assembly all dedicated to the destruction of Tokyo and Japan. At night, the phosphorescence of the water all around us was all that was visible of this stupendous array of warships.

This "handbook to life" is a brilliantly evocative, scrupulously honest, and extremely well-written description of naval life on the lower deck in World War II, comparable only, so far as I know, to the equally distinguished memoir of another aviator turned scholar, Samuel Hynes. If anyone wants to know what it was really like to serve in the U.S. Navy in World War II, these are the books to read.

Lawrence Stone

PREFACE TO THE YALE EDITION

The first publication of *Crossing the Line* in 1994 brought a flood of welcome letters from people who remembered the events I described as intensely as I did. "How young we were," said most, and some brought me new information, such as how Al Capone's bullet-proof Cadillac limo got to Shanghai to provide transportation for the commanding officer. Others had different views of events from those I remembered. An intelligence officer wrote that my story about the plans for Midway circulating by scuttlebutt on the *Enterprise* a month before the battle simply could not have been true since it was the war's best-kept secret. I could only reply that on this matter my memory was firm and clear. Years afterward a discussion of the matter on the online Battle of Midway Round Table revealed that numerous people knew that we had the names of the Japanese ships and the battle plans. Cincpac, authorized by Admiral Nimitz, before the battle had sent out both an ULTRA radio communication and a standard coded description of the Japanese battle plans. The information was discussed at meetings in wardrooms, published on bulletin boards, and given to flight crews.

Vice Admiral William D. Houser, USN (Ret.), wrote that he had been in the antiaircraft batteries on the USS *Nashville* when it fired on the Japanese picket boats encountered as the *Hornet* was about to launch the Doolittle raiders on Tokyo. I had referred to the failure of a thousand six-inch shells to sink the pickets as "disgraceful." Vice Admiral Houser took exception to this term, explaining that "*Nashville* opened fire at long range on the wildly tossing craft and scored a number of hits. The gunfire straddled the small wooden ship but the shells were all armor piercing (AP) and thus hits passed through without exploding." Vice Admiral

Houser also sent a copy of his letter and my book to Rear Admiral Harry Mason, USN (Ret.), who just happened to have been the fire control officer on the *Nashville* that day. He thought my story sounded like it had been told by Sinbad the Sailor or by my old ordnance chief, Murphy, befuddled by drinking his "moosemilk" compounded of coffee and bombsight alcohol.

In time the mail brought a book, too, Steve Ewing and John Lundstrom's *Fatal Rendezvous: The Life of Butch O'Hare* (1997), containing a thorough investigation of the night-fighter flight on which O'Hare was killed. Over the years a story had grown that I had shot O'Hare down, but Ewing and Lundstrom concluded that he had fallen to enemy fire. Understandably, this greatly relieved the guilt that I had carried over the years about the possibility that I had hit the group commander while firing at the Japanese intruder.

Most of the communications came from shipmates of half a century ago who had stored away in their heads some of the same scenes I had in mine. Imagine opening a letter to read, "I recall you and I up on the hangar deck of CV-8 [the sinking *Hornet*] waiting to climb down the cargo net to the deck of the DD410, *Hughes*. I recall, while in line, you asked me if there was anything I wanted from my locker. I said, 'Kernan, I wouldn't go back for anything.' You insisted on going—you came back with a pillow cover with my gear." This was my old shipmate Dan Vanderhoof, not seen or heard from for fifty years. Some voices came back from the dead. I had written about three bodies stretched out on the deck of the USS *Suwanee* after one of their own hundred-pound bombs hung up, armed in their bomb bay, and exploded on landing. Then came a letter from Dick Morrow, the gunner, who had spent a long and prosperous life directing a fashionable dance band in the suburbs of Detroit: "I had no idea what had happened until the flames began to burn me. . . . I remember releasing the turret window latch and fell out. . . . I also remember hearing over the ship's loudspeaker 'Taps' at the moment Obie [the pilot,

Lt. (jg) O. B. Slingerland] was being buried at sea. . . . Then while on a landing barge I heard a medical corpsman exclaim that [the radioman] Jim Joyce's tongue was swollen and he had passed away."

Often children whose fathers had mentioned only brief events in the war wrote to find out what it had actually been like the day the *Hornet* sank, or what the scene looked like when Lieutenant Collura went down on the way back from Ishigaki. Occasionally relatives who had never heard how men I mentioned had died wrote to ask for information: "I am the widow of John Wiley Brock, who was . . . in VT-6 on the old *Enterprise,* and was killed in 1942 at Midway. . . . What I would like to know is do you remember him? I have never found anyone who did. I would like this information for our son . . . who never knew his father."

This book was originally published by the Naval Institute Press in 1994, in paper in 1997. I am most grateful to the Institute for the fine treatment they gave the book and the skill with which they promoted it over the years. Largely because of the responses to the book like those described above, I was unwilling, however, to see it go out of print, and the Naval Institute very generously returned the copyright, making it possible for me to publish this new edition with Yale University Press. I want to thank the Naval Historical Center for many of the illustrations, which they generously have placed in the public domain.

Crossing the Line

ONE

Snow

In the winter of 1940–41, I stood in the deep snows of the mountains of southern Wyoming and realized that it wasn't going to work. Our ranch was five miles from the nearest neighbor, and during the winter months we had to snowshoe or ski that five miles, leaving the car where the county snowplow had stopped, carrying in packs or pulling on sleds whatever was necessary until the next month, when we would go to town again—Saratoga, about twenty miles away. We would cut enough wood in summer to keep the stoves burning and store enough staples in a frost-proof cave dug into the mountainside to see us through the winter. There was no electricity or running water. The horses were driven down the valley and boarded for the winter with people who lived out of the shadow of the mountain, where the snows were the heaviest. The cats were brown and singed on their sides from spending their days trying to keep warm curled around the stovepipes that came out of the roof.

The ranch had been one of the last homesteads taken out and "proved up," 640 acres in a canyon near the head of South Spring Creek, 8,500 feet high, a few miles east of the crest of the Continental Divide. The stream flowed down into the valley of the North Platte and into the young river that comes out of the Colorado mountains. It was a very real place—water, sagebrush, rocks, pine trees—but the ranch was also a dream, my stepfather's dream, after he lost his work in the Depression, that a Wyoming dude ranch would provide a wonderful life for all of us and eventually make us rich. As in many other American families during the Depression, conversations frequently began with, "When we get rich . . ." The ranch had made us neither rich nor happy, and there was never the slightest chance that it would, with no building capital, few fish and little big game, and no dudes with enough money or interest to find their way to a small rundown ranch forty miles from a railroad or a main highway. My stepfather couldn't see it, of course; he had no place else to go. But my sense that things were going wrong had been growing since the evening of September 1, 1939, when we listened to the news, on a radio powered by an old car battery, that Hitler had invaded Poland, and that Britain and France had declared war. We knew, sadly, far away though it was, that it would affect us, and that life would never again be the same. But nothing much changed until I graduated from high school in 1940. I had boarded in town while I went to school, but now, unable to get a job, I was staying on the ranch alone, taking care of things, and had to face the question of how I was going to live my life. My stepfather was away in the East looking for work, my mother with him.

In early November, I got a heads-up about how life really works. The snows had held off longer than usual, and I had delayed taking the horses down below. One day an old car, a Star coupe, a model by then no longer sold or familiar, pulled up and stopped in front of the fence, waiting. No one got out for a while. In that time and place it was not thought polite to be too forward, and I waited before going down to lean on the fence, establishing ownership, and say hello. By then two men and a pregnant woman had gotten out of the car. They wanted to know the condition of the road above our ranch, a road that ran for about ten miles through the Medicine Bow National Forest up to South Spring Creek Lake. The lake was in the core of an old volcano with one side blown out, Mount Saint

Helens fashion, out of which ran South Spring Creek down the canyon in which our ranch was located. The road, built years ago and poorly maintained, was at the best of times unimproved, running over big rocks, through swamps, dugways nearly washed away in the side of mountains, across rotting log bridges, and, in places, up 40-degree slopes. I told the strangers that the bridges, though shaky, had all still been there a week ago when I had gone deer hunting up that way, but that they would need something powerful and high centered to get up the road, all things their antique car was not. They went off together and talked for a while, and then came back and asked if I would take them by wagon to an old mine up on the shoulder of Mount Vulcan, rising high on one side of the lake. They were out-of-work miners, hoping to find a mine and work it for enough ore to sell to a smelter in Colorado to keep going, always with the hope of a real strike. We were all dreamers then.

The weather was not good: the snow was likely to begin any time, which I explained to them, adding truthfully that once it began at this time of year, you could get snowed in all winter. They still wanted to go, and I sensed that there might be real money in this job, so I gulped and said I would go for ten dollars. I had never had ten dollars at once, and they too were impressed with the big bucks we were talking. Since they were nearly broke, they bargained hard, starting at five dollars, moving to seven, and agreeing to ten only when I, knowing nothing about bargaining, remained adamant, on condition that I feed them, let them sleep there that night, and allow the pregnant woman to stay in the cabin while we were gone.

Feeling like a real trader, I had the old team hitched to the wagon the next morning before light, with some oats for them in a sack, and off we went, with the smell of snow in the air. We jolted along, and I worried about whether my stepfather would ever find out, and if he did, whether he would want half of the money for wear and tear on the horses and the wagon, or whether he would just be plain mad about my doing something with his property without permission. He and I didn't agree about a lot of things.

With enough snow on the ground to make the rocks slick, the going was slower than usual, and at that time of year dark came in the deepening canyon by four in the afternoon. Shortly after a lunchless noon, we got stuck in a narrow place trying to turn between some rocks. The wagon box was sixteen feet long and firmly wedged; a shorter one would have been much better for this work. After some geeing and hawing it was clear that the only way to get out of there was to unhitch the horses, take off the wagon box, disassemble the wagon, and put it together facing the opposite way, downhill and back toward the ranch. The miners weren't happy with this. "Isn't there some way to get to the mine and get the drills without using the wagon?" There was a back trail leading directly to the mine, up the ridge and across the shoulder of the mountain; but the only way to bring the heavy drills out would be to hook them to the harness traces on the horses and drag them along, bouncing up and down on the rocks, careering down the slopes. "That's okay; rock drills are tough anyway." So up through the fading light, soft snow drifting down, high up on the shoulder of the green mountain, we made our way through the pines to the old mine. A spooky place, abandoned years ago, leaving behind a diesel engine, compressor, drills, and a lot of other equipment. We hooked a drill to each horse and started back down the mountain. Dark set in and the snow increased, big heavy wet white flakes, not quite a blizzard, but not reassuring either.

By the time we got back to the wagon it was pitch dark, and time for the strenuous work of getting the wagon, locked into the rocks in the big pine grove, apart and back together facing the other way. We should have done it before going up the mountain, but the miners had been in a hurry. Now it had to be done in the dark. The miners wanted to build a fire and get warm, but I argued that things were getting tight, and it was time to work hard and get the hell out of there. They went ahead building a fire, saying that they had hired me and the wagon, and it was my problem to get them back. Angry enough to be able to do it, I got the box out of the bolsters onto a rock, took the reach out, reversed the wheels, and put the box back in.

The miners got in sullenly and hunched down in their coats. I couldn't see a thing, and let the horses find the way, which was fine until we came to a bridge they didn't like. They spooked, backed and snorted, the harness rattling and jangling, and wouldn't go on. I got down and took hold of the mare's bridle and led them across the bridge. It seemed easier on foot, so I continued walking, leading the horses and talking to them. About eleven at night we got back to the ranch. The miners went up to the cabin, and I took the horses to the barn. By the time I had unharnessed and fed the horses, the miners and the woman were piling things in the car, saying they wanted to get out of there before the snow—by then about six inches deep—made it impossible to get up a steep hill on the only road out of the canyon. That was fine with me, I had seen enough of them, but nothing was said about the ten dollars as they piled into the car. I was prepared to fight for it after the day I'd just had. In fact, I was going to make it impossible for them to get out of there, and they must have felt the growing tension, for at the last minute they handed over an old, dirty ten dollar bill, got in the car, and roared out.

The futility of it all was underlined the following summer, after I was gone, when they came back with an old Fordson tractor with a compressor on the back that they were taking up to the mine, planning to work it. They stopped to talk to my stepfather for a while, and he heard for the first time what had happened the winter before, but when they got ready to go, the hand-cranked tractor wouldn't start. They cranked it for a day and a half, no exaggeration, taking turns, before it fired. Then they clanked out, but about a hundred yards up the road the steering gear broke in a deep rut. There was a power reel on the front of the tractor with a hundred feet of cable, and from there on—the whole ten miles or so up that canyon, over those rocks, to the mine—they reeled out the cable, fastened the end to a tree, then winched the tractor up by its own bootstraps, as it were, to the tree, where the same job began all over again.

These later disasters merely drove home what the miners had already taught me on that long November day about the futility of life lived with old, broken-down equipment, about foolish ideas that have no chance of succeeding. In a world where disaster is always ready to happen, it is best to look for something that has a chance of working. And after the miners left the winter came on in earnest. A wind that would knock you off your feet, snow eight feet deep, and weeks of below zero weather put a still finer edge on my thinking. Seventeen years old, no job, no prospects, I knew how to do only one thing, the same thing all inland mountain boys do, go to sea. I think my parents were glad to see me go; one less pair of hands but also one less mouth to feed—one less worry, it seemed at the time, about what was going to happen. They were a little ashamed of not having been able to send me to college or provide a paying job for me, but nobody had helped them out, and they were, I thought, glad I had relieved them of their vague feelings of guilt and responsibility.

And so one day in March, with heavy snow clouds hanging gray over the ranch, I borrowed five dollars—having long ago spent my profits from the trip to the mine—and got a ride down to Cheyenne. A ground blizzard was blowing on U.S. 30 from Rawlins to Cheyenne. Blazing bright sunlight and blue sky above, snow blowing a few inches above the ground so thickly that it was as impossible to see the road as it was to see my future.

I found the recruiting center in the Cheyenne post office and signed up for a minority enlistment (until I was twenty-one years old) in the United States Navy. The train went down to Denver that evening. There, in a room in Union Station, about a hundred young men were assembled from all over the Rocky Mountains to take the oath. We were young—

seventeen, eighteen, nineteen—and for the most part, kids who couldn't get jobs. Here and there were men in their twenties, jobless workers at the end of their rope, or incorrigible "fuck-ups" who had gotten into some kind of trouble at home once too often and had been given the ancient choice by the judge of going to jail or joining one of the services. Most of us were from small towns, often from broken families, notable for bad teeth and worse complexions, the marginal American products of more than ten years of the hardest of times.

After the oath we went out to the cold platform and into the warm cars. Not expecting anything other than coaches, we murmured our pleasure at the sleeping berths the navy provided its newest members. The yellow Union Pacific train, with its streamlined engine and coaches, snaked through long curves out of the Colorado and New Mexico plateaus, across the mountains, to stop in the bright sunshine of California on the second morning. The warmth itself was luxurious after the cold of the mountains, and the orange groves and Spanish architecture seemed to promise the freedom and pleasure that I had longed for in the deep snows of Wyoming. A glimpse of Los Angeles, Union Station, and then the train rounded a bend and there was the Pacific Ocean, blue and infinite, the sea of adventure and excitement, stretching out to the horizon and beyond: Hawaii, the Philippines, Indonesia, China, and Japan. I would see them all, I was sure, and in time I did, but not quite as I imagined them in that moment of wild surmise.

TWO

Boots

The U.S. Naval Training Station, San Diego, was in 1941 the boot camp for all those who enlisted in the mountain region and the West Coast. Stuck out next to the marine boot camp on a beach extending in a westerly curve to Point Loma, forming the northwestern shore of San Diego Bay, the camp faced the Naval Air Station on North Island across the water. The huge harbor and its shores were the training center for the Pacific Fleet, which was now home ported at Pearl Harbor in the Hawaiian Islands. Inside the main gate of the training station two-story stucco barracks with arcades stretched out in long rows to the blacktop "grinder," the drill field where we would spend most of the next few months learning the naval axiom that military duties take precedence over trade skills by marching as a company, under arms, back and forth, up and down, on the oblique, to the rear, rear, rear, march!

Soft warm air, light breezes, and the lift that intense sunlight gives: the climate had a holiday feel even in those strenuous first days of boot camp, which began with a physical exam, where the city boys laughed at those of us from the country still wearing long underwear. Since my long johns came only to the waist, with a T-shirt above, I thought myself quite sophisticated, but this was still far from the West Coast jockey-short style, and I was glad to package the underwear with my other clothes—

the Hart, Schafner, and Marx suit bought as a high school graduation present, my stepfather's cut-down topcoat, the gray hat—to be sent home. Civilian identity vanished with the clothes, and, naked, we were initiated into our new identities, which were minimal, by probing, poking, testing, shooting. The barbers sheared off almost all our hair, leaving only an inch on top, bare on the sides. For some the loss of long, carefully groomed hair was as painful as it was to Samson, but to most of us it was only a necessary part of becoming a sailor.

Once out of the barbershop we counted off, and when the number reached one hundred, two chief petty officers advanced purposefully and claimed us as a company. Chief Dahlgren was a gunner's mate, tall, tolerant, composed, Nordic. Chief Bilbo was a short, stocky, fiery, Sicilian and truly dangerous to disappoint. Company 41-39 was the thirty-ninth company formed at San Diego in 1941, and after being assigned a barracks it was marched off to stores, where the navy issued the clothes and equipment needed to live in and work with from then on.

Whap! The heavy canvas hammock landed on the brightly polished, red linoleum deck (no longer a floor) in front of each man, who then dragged it along in front of the counters where endless items were called out—"Two undress uniforms, white, one pair of leggings canvas, khaki"— and thrown on the hammock. Sea bag for all clothing, ditty bag for toilet gear and personal possessions. Dress blues (one) with a white watchstander's qualification stripe around the right shoulder to identify you as a deckhand, not a red-striped engineer, and one white tape around the cuffs to mark you as the lowest of all beings in the navy, an apprentice seaman. Black silk neckerchiefs (two) to be folded into a long flat ribbon and tied around the neck with a square knot exactly at the bottom of the vee in the blouse. Undress blues, no tape on collar and uncuffed sleeves; dungarees for work details; white caps and blue wool flat cap; pea coat (to be paid for from pay in installments); one pair of low dress shoes. "What's your size?"

The pile on the hammock grew mountainous: smallclothes (underwear), line for lashing hammock, cord for hanging washed clothes up to dry, a flat mattress and two covers, pillow, shoe brush and dauber, socks, black and white. At the end of the line two sailors grabbed the hammock, folded it double, put the rings on either end in your hand and hoisted it onto your back. Bent double with this huge white hump on your back, you followed the arrows and your company number chalked on the sidewalk to the barracks, where you were assigned to a double-deck bunk and began to fold, tie, and store your clothing in your sea bag.

There was little personal gear. The navy did not encourage private possessions. A pocketknife was allowed, as were scissors, toothbrush, razor, soap, shoe polish, and some writing materials. These were kept in the ditty bag tied to the side of your bunk. There wasn't room for anything else and no place elsewhere to stow anything. In time, on shipboard, the sea bag and ditty bag gave way to a small locker, but in training the Old Navy tradition of little gear packed compactly in tight quarters survived. Clothing was folded and stored. Each piece, from jumpers to skivvies, was folded in a particular way, rolled tightly, and then tied with white clothes stops, square knotted at a prescribed point, the cord ending in a brass collar just at the knot. No "Irish pennants" (loose ends) allowed here. The folds for storage gave the uniforms their distinctive appearance when worn, like the three ridges on the collar of the blue-and-white jumpers or the inverse seam on the trousers from being stored inside out.

No dirt. Cleanliness was not next to godliness in the United States Navy; it was godliness. Everything in the barracks was constantly shined to a high gloss, from the red linoleum floors to the brass work on the fire hose fittings. Shoes were a brilliant deep black, in contrast with the unspotted white uniforms that we scrubbed every day, kneeling with a stiff brush and harsh soap on the cement platforms provided for that purpose in the rear of the barracks.

Men were expected to be as clean as their quarters and equipment, and most were so by easy choice. Company 41-39 contained, inevitably, one of those odd people encountered here and there in every walk of life who not only smell foul by nature, it seems, but nurture the smell by keeping themselves and their clothes as dirty as possible. Pigpen in the comic strip "Peanuts" is an attractive version of this human oddity. Our Pigpen stuffed his sea bag with dirty clothes, never brushed his teeth or washed, and lay in his bunk with one hand under the blanket (forbidden by unwritten rule), giggling, reading a comic book. The remedy was gleeful and brutal. From time to time he was stripped and put in the wash trough, surrounded by jeering recruits, secure in their own cleanliness, who washed him down with a gritty sand soap and then scrubbed him with stiff long-handled brushes. The process, which involved a lot of hitting with the brush handles, was painful, a form of running the gauntlet, but it never had the slightest effect. Nowadays he would have sued the navy, but when I last saw Pigpen he was lying in his bunk, smelling horrible, one hand under the blanket, giggling and reading the same page of the comic book he had been looking at when I first staggered into the barracks under my load of equipment. I thought then that he must always have been there, and he probably still is, some old Adam who haunts all the navy's efforts at cleanliness, positive thinking, and order.

We were children still—astonishingly stoical, self-reliant, tough children, but children still—and, like all children, fascinated with killing. The guns drew us like magnets when they were given to us one afternoon in the huge, cool armory, filled with the odor of greasy brown cosmolene, where each of us was issued, and signed our life away for, a rifle. Stands of boarding cutlasses still stood as ornaments next to the cases of rifles, but so innocent were we that we thought boarding enemy vessels—just like Errol Flynn in the movies set on the Spanish Main—was still a part of naval warfare and were disappointed when we had to be satisfied with only a murderous sixteen-inch bayonet.

Springfield rifles, 1903, .30 caliber, were the standard issue, but every seventh unlucky company (and the lot fell on 41-39) was given British-made long Enfields from the First World War. The Enfield weighed three pounds more than the Springfield, and we soon found out just what those three pounds meant at the end of a long, hot ten hours on the grinder. Not only that, you lived with that heavy rifle in boot camp, using it in morning calisthenics, running around the grinder with it at high port for punishment, slamming it around your head and shoulders with one hand while going through the manual of arms. In the end you were stronger for having lugged that extra three pounds about with you, but Atlas could have been no gladder to get rid of his load than we were when we finally gave those huge, heavy guns back to the armory.

The grinder was where we learned the really hard lesson of military life: putting your individuality in storage and moving as a group. On ten or more acres of baking black asphalt, shimmering with heat waves in the hot afternoon sun of the Mexican border, the company marched as a unit—white hats turned down to protect nose and neck from sunburn—five days a week, inspection on Saturday, up and down, by the right flank, by the left flank, to the rear, march! Eyes right, eyes left, eyes front, right shoulder arms, left shoulder arms. In four columns, tallest men at front. Blessed were the shortest, for no one marched behind them; they were always getting out of step and scraping their well-polished heels with the out-of-step toes of their shoes. Not only was it infuriating, hot, and exhausting to be stepped on by some bastard who couldn't keep step—and there were those congenitally unable to do so—but it also scuffed the backs of the shoes, making it impossible to polish them smoothly and deeply again, which led to trouble at the next inspection. Reasonable excuses were not a part of this life. The company would be moving smoothly along, the Olympian Dahlgren at front, a sword on his shoulder, Bilbo at the rear, shouting time: "Hut, two, three, four, and your left, your right, your left, goddammit!" Then a shout, "You dirty son of a bitch," and turmoil would break out in the middle of the ranks, a few blows. Someone had, once again, stepped on somebody's heels "for the last time." The company would halt, order would be restored, punishments handed out, and off we would go, "Your left, your right, your left, hold up your fucking heads."

After fifty years, the only name I remember from this group with whom I lived so intimately for three months is Mudrick, the man who marched immediately behind me, had trouble keeping step, whined a lot, and filled my heart with red murder on those blazing afternoons when he stepped on my heels again and again and snickered when I muttered oaths. Years later there was a cross-grained literary critic named Marvin Mudrick, whom I never knew, but whom I loathed on the unlikely suspicion that he must be the same man, up to his old trick of being out of step.

Money was no problem because we had none. The few coins that everyone hoarded were saved for cigarettes—it was part of manhood to smoke at that time—which could be bought during a once-weekly few minutes in the ship's store at the duty-free price of five cents a package. There was no time to smoke during the day, and the smoking lamp was always out in the barracks. But during the evening while outdoors washing clothes, the fortunate few with cigarettes could light up. Their pleasure was lessened a great deal by the envious faces that peered at them as intently as begging dogs. As soon as they took the pack out of the sleeve of the skivvy shirt, where it was twisted up to keep the cigarettes from being dampened by sweat, a loud cry of "butts" would come from the throat of some wretch whose need for nicotine had overwhelmed self-pride. The cry was privileged, and as soon as the first smoker had smoked his fill, he had to turn over the butt to the man who had claimed it rather than putting it in the sand bucket. Usually the man who had been "butted" couldn't take the hungry look of the "butter" and smoked the cigarette down only halfway before giving up in disgust. As time passed between paydays and fewer had cigarettes, the sound of "butts" would be followed by the desperate call of "butts on the butts!" "Butts on the butts on the butts" was only a joke, but there were those who would have tried it if social opinion would have tolerated it.

"Twenty-one dollars a day, once a month" was the refrain of an old song, and twenty-one dollars a month was the pay of apprentice seamen. The navy didn't bother paying at the end of the first month in boot camp, on the theory that you had no need of money since you couldn't go on liberty until the end of the second month. But at the end of the second month the solemn naval ritual of payday began with the posting of the pay lists a few days before payday. All to be paid were on the list with first, second, and third names. If you lacked a middle name, the navy, sure that all humans needed a middle name for purposes of identification, supplied one: None. None was the most frequent middle name in the navy, and Samuel None Jones or Fred None Smith would be followed by the amount the navy figured it owed you after all the deductions were made. A legendary recruit joined the navy with only the name J. B. He soon became Jonly Bonly.

The amount was always less than the sailor calculated he had coming to him. This was why the lists were posted beforehand, so that the arguments could be sorted out before you passed, neatly dressed in the uniform of the day, in alphabetical order down the line in front of the yeomen and that august figure, the warrant paymaster. If you were going home on leave after boot camp, money was deducted to pay for your train ticket, the heavy pea coat, and any fines or punishments. Also allotments. You wouldn't think there would be anything to spare out of twenty-one dollars minus deductions, but there were men whose families were so poor that they would send them ten dollars, or even more, every month. And then, at the end of the line, looking particularly grim, Bilbo and Dahlgren would be standing behind the Red Cross and the Navy Relief representatives, each of whom had to be given a dollar if you wanted to avoid getting on the company's permanent shit list, which brought all kinds of drab extra work. Lifelong dislikes of the Red Cross were born in front of the superior-looking, elegantly uniformed lady who disdainfully took your dollar while chatting with one of the supervising officers. But Navy Relief, which provided for families of enlisted men fallen on hard times, was accepted as a tax on life. The families of enlisted men in peacetime had an Appalachian quality to them at best, so grim as to make us both sorry for them and determined while in service to avoid marriage and children at all costs.

There were always navy ships in San Diego Harbor, and on the first liberty, Saturday from noon to ten o'clock, they drew me, along with many others, across the bay to the North Island docks to spend a fireman's holiday going from one great ship to another. The aircraft carrier *Lexington,* blocks long and tall as a hotel, was irresistible. We asked the officer-of-the-deck permission to come aboard—"Permission granted"—and saluted toward the rear of the ship, where the flag was flown at anchor, in the manner we had learned in *The Bluejackets' Manual.* With a few smiles at our oversize boot uniforms and rounded hats, we were allowed to wander about looking at the planes on the hangar deck and the guns, small and large, around the immense flight deck. The high smokestack with ladder rungs welded to the side was so tempting that I climbed up to near the top, getting more and more scared at the height, until someone called from below telling me to get the hell off.

The streetcar clanged back to "Dago" where the streets were filled with sailors on liberty. The bars, with someone sitting on a stool at each door to examine your liberty card to make sure you were twenty-one, stood with their doors open and the jukeboxes blaring out "Hut sut rawson on the rilliraw" and "Drinking rum and coca cola, Working for the Yankee dollar." Neon lights flashed over "The Arabian Palace Hotel" and "Intimate Nights," where the Shore Patrol stood on the sidewalks swinging their clubs and looking mean, and the smell of Lysol hung in the air. In the tattoo parlors, open to the street, sailors were getting dragons, daggers, and

"Death before Dishonor" worked in vivid color on their arms and backs, the bright inks mixed with sweat and blood standing in pools, shining in the bright lights. Of all the walkers on the streets, only the boots with floppy white-issue uniforms and broad white hats sitting squarely on the head, the brim flaring wide out, neckerchiefs tied at the vee of the jumper rather than at the throat, looked like real rubes. Everyone else looked in the know: tight uniforms, campaign ribbons, old chief boatswains' mates from the Asiatic station, and long-term hands with rows of hash marks on their sleeves.

There was real, vulgar joy among so much life ordered by a symbology of hierarchy and skill that flashed along the streets. Petty officers with rating badges displayed on the left arm for the trades, on the right for those who worked on deck like quartermasters, gunners, and coxswains. Red hash marks on most, gold hash marks after twelve years of consecutive good conduct. White uniforms, dress blues, khakis, and greens here and there on the aviation chiefs. Lots of sailors were in civvies, usually a garish Hawaiian or Philippine shirt, with tight trousers and cheap boots that were kept, along with a bottle, in locker clubs, where for a few bucks you could drink, shower, and change clothes for liberty. Selling uniforms and badges was big business. Outside each clothing store an affable man called out, "Hey, chief!" to every sailor who walked by, trying to lure them into buying tight-fitting tailor-made uniforms, gold dragons stitched into the silk lining of the panel above the crotch. "Liberty" was the right word for it. It was an enlisted man's world on the streets; the officers, unenvied, stayed with their strained-looking women in the hotels or in Coronado in one of the officers' clubs.

In time basic training ended. Those who were going straight to the fleet without further training to become deckhands and firemen were given a ten-day leave, and with any luck had saved enough money to pay for a train ticket home. The rest of us went off to another three months in a training school to learn a trade. It was necessary to pass some rudimentary exams to be accepted for one of the training schools, but since promotion came more rapidly to those with a trade and the work was easier, schools were thought desirable. The great reason for joining the navy in those Depression days was to learn a trade. But it wasn't anything so practical that directed my choice. Out of all the useful skills I could have learned—radio, electricity, motors, signaling, navigation, even boiler making—I, wild about flying and airplanes, chose aviation ordnance, bombs, aerial torpedoes, machine guns, and other instruments of destruction. This was thought a good route to flying as a gunner or an observer, even to pilot training, and this is what I was after.

With our sea bags lashed up in our hammocks and on our shoulders, looking like real seamen for the first time, we walked up the hill to the holding barracks for the long row of training schools. Here you stayed until enough people arrived in your specialty to form a class, and in the meantime the navy found work to busy idle hands. The barracks were new and built about three feet off the ground on spaced cement pilings. Someone had had the idea that it would be good to fill the empty space with dirt dug from the clay hill behind the barracks. Just why was never explained. The dirt was dragged in baskets by hand to the center of the area, dumped, and pushed back.

It was dirty and hard work, and I was delighted when the chief in charge of the barracks selected me and one other young sailor to clean his room. The room was only about ten by six, with a bunk, a chair, and a locker, and one person, let alone two, could have kept it spotless working about half an hour a day. Innocent as lambs, both of us looking very young, the other sailor and I never questioned our good fortune, slicking up the room, running a few errands, and then loafing in the ship's store or reading in out-of-the-way areas. I don't think I had ever heard of homosexuality, and when the chief, having sent the other cleaner off on an errand, made his smiling, good-natured move, I was so aghast that I jumped without thinking in one giant leap out the open window, which fortunately was on the first floor. No hard feelings, but within the hour I was back on the dirt gang with the worst job, at the front of the line pushing the dirt by hand close to the barrack's floor.

In a few days the class for aviation ordnance school filled up, and we moved to another barracks, double-decker bunks on each side, with a long desk made of two planks, with fixed benches, running down the center for study. Light and clean, simple but efficient, it was a pleasant place to spend the late summer and fall of 1941. The course itself was easy—a few simple facts about electricity and some rudimentary chemistry, learning the difference between one type of bomb rack and another, some information about various explosives and the fuses used to ignite them, how to break down, clean, and adjust machine guns, pistols, and rifles. Probably the most complicated mechanism was the aerial torpedo, which ran on an ingenious little steam engine fired by alcohol and contained a lot of complex gyroscopes and settings to control depths and angles. At the Battle of Midway I would learn that our aerial torpedo, Mark 13, Mod. 1, was deeply flawed, seldom running hot and true and regularly failing to explode. But like all the fairly crude weaponry we worked on, it seemed to be the latest martial technology, to be studied with care.

We saw no real airplanes in training school; instead, we bore sighted machine guns (that is, aligned them to converge their fire at a certain number of yards in front of the plane) on a frame model of an old plane. Learning on a mock-up to synchronize machine guns so that they could fire through a turning propeller without hitting the blades, we made a gambling game out of whether the firing solenoid clicked on empty space or on an old propeller turned slowly by hand.

Twelve-hour liberties were given on three out of four weekends. On the fourth your section had the watch. By now we had become second-class seamen, with a pay raise from twenty-one to thirty-six dollars a month, which meant that for the first time that we had some real money left over after deductions when we were paid every two weeks. Everyone bought a small black wallet designed to tuck without much bulge into a uniform waistband or into the small breast pocket on the jumper.

Before the war the navy had the quaint custom of paying in two-dollar bills, perhaps because no one else wanted them, but the sailors all said it was because two dollars was what they charged in the whorehouses in Dago. In a small town crowded with sailors, life moved from the bars to the whorehouses and back to the bars. Eighteen-year-olds like myself, with little cash, were not very welcome in either, even with doctored identification, but no one really worried much, and sooner or later you could work your way into a bar to sit with your friends, eight or ten in a booth, and tell stories about what a good job you had had back in civilian life, how much money you had made, your flashy clothes and car, the adoring and obliging girlfriends. Having had none of these I listened happily to the more polished liars, kept time to the music of the jukebox, and basked in the sense of being one of a group of real men of the world.

The local beer was the drink, cheap and sufficient for inexperienced drinkers like myself, but sometimes money would be pooled to buy a pint of some bright-colored gin—sloe, mint, apricot—more memorable for its vividness coming up than its pleasure going down, and with this in a paper bag we would sit on the curb, or, sometimes, five or six together, take a room in one of the whorehouses. A quirk of the law required them actually to rent rooms, which they did for a few dollars, and groups of sailors would take one to sit in drinking and talking to the whores, strongly perfumed, who came in from time to time for a drink and to see if there was any business.

You could also sit in the parlors for a limited time looking at the girls in scanty costumes who displayed themselves provocatively, and then move on to another house, and another. It was all incredibly garish and tawdry; most people would probably think the strong sounds and smells vulgar, even disgusting, but to young men in their late teens, with their experience of women limited for the most part to a few awkward pawings in a parked automobile, their glands in an uproar, and their sexual urgencies flowing full tide, it looked like Babylon itself, the harem of the sultans, the paradise of the true believers. The Oriental motif carried on to a pale, slender young girl called Cleo, who with good humor and real tenderness took me through my sexual initiation on a sagging old bed in a quiet room, jukebox music in the distance and a cool breeze playing gently over our bodies from the electric fan. It was not a romantic setting, far from it—sensible and workmanlike, rather—but it was not brutal or degrading for anyone.

Later, on the stairs going out, I heard a drunken sailor who had gotten into an argument with a whore cursing the madam. She screamed back at him, "You want to hurt someone? You fucking cocksucker. Come on and fuck me, and I'll show you how to hurt someone fucking." This had nothing to do with me or the sex I had just found in Cleo's thin arms, and I hurried on out to the bus back to the base, where, after the liberty card was deposited in the box, reality spoke up again in the prophylactic station where you were required to pump some stinging brown liquid up your cock—sometimes fainting when you did so if you had had too much to drink—washed, and used an antiseptic cream. Gonorrhea was endemic in the fleet, and fearful tales went around of syphilis picked up in the Orient, requiring long, painful treatment and spinal taps and eventuating in various kinds of rot and disintegration.

For someone with a good memory and a feel for simple systems, the training school was easy, but for others it was a slow drudgery, involving sitting up in the heads all night to try to get the facts down for one of the dreaded weekly exams. Not everyone in the school was a genius. One sailor was a boxer, and he practiced sometimes by sparring with one of the iron support posts in the middle of the barracks. He would get very excited at times, so much so that he would bang his head on the post until one of us told him to break, that the round had ended. He and some others flunked out, but most passed, and all through the war I ran into them in odd places in the Pacific, filling practice bombs with sand on Guadalcanal, caring for ammunition storage depots on Ford Island, taking the temperatures in the bomb magazines of aircraft carriers like the *Hornet,* cleaning machine guns on a racetrack in New Caledonia, and loading bombs in Okinawa.

I was the honor man of the class, not because of my mechanical skills—I was a bit clumsy—but because of the written tests. The chief in charge of our class arranging graduation ceremonies had never laid eyes on me and did not know my name, so when he called it out to tell me to go up on stage, he had to ask someone, "Who is he?" This was a mark of great success to me and to my friends: you did your work and got ahead but remained totally anonymous. This is how you survived in the navy and most other places in the world before the modern triumph of the cult of personality. At those graduation ceremonies on October 21, 1941, I shook hands for the first time with a commissioned officer, creatures seen only from a distance theretofore. Captain Henry Gearing was the commander of the U.S. Naval Training Station, San Diego, a grizzled old sea dog, at least in appearance, bluff, tall, commanding. When he saw me on the stage, small and thin and still very young-looking, he leaned over and whispered as he gave me the diploma, "My God, boy, how old are you?" I thought I had set his concerns entirely at ease by truthfully answering, "Eighteen," having reached that advanced age in June, and went out to the tune of "Anchors Aweigh" for fifteen days of leave at home.

Two days of sitting up on a train so packed there was not even any standing room left returned me to the cold of Wyoming. Rawlins, where the train stopped, is sixty miles from our ranch across the bleak desert of south-central Wyoming. Up in the mountains a few inches of snow had already fallen by the end of October; the yellow leaves were all gone from the aspens, and at the line where they ended and the green pines began the dark and cold of winter were already to be felt. The mountains rose up and up through the pines to the bare space above timberline. Their bald peaks dominated our ranch, loomed over everything with menacing size and durability. They set the scale of reality here, of things as they permanently are, and against them everything else seemed ephemeral and puny. The new cabin with the stone fireplace, for the dudes who would never come, the ranch itself and all the hopes invested in it, the faraway sunniness of California, where nature seems to promise a lot, and even the might of the United States Navy were emptied of reality by those monstrous mountains and the oncoming winter.

I had expected to return a hero, and the dog was glad to see me, and my mother fussed over me and listened with real interest to my stories. My stepfather, who had not seen service in the First World War, felt somewhat threatened by my military authority and constantly told me there wouldn't be a war. But my life and interests had migrated elsewhere, and, half aware of it, I had some guilt for not feeling the old loyalties. A brief trip to Saratoga, where nothing had happened since I left and where no one was interested in my adventures, was only awkward.

That was the last time I saw my mother alive, and as I write this, almost exactly fifty years later, I am troubled by how little I can remember of her, barely able to see her worried face in the lamplight or hear her words of good advice as I left. The big snows held off, and in early November 1941 they drove me back to the train that took me to the bustle of San Diego and on to Pearl Harbor and the other side of the world.

THREE

Pearl

The USS *Procyon,* a military cargo vessel, sailed from San Diego to Pearl Harbor in mid-November 1941, loaded with various stores and machines and packed with sailors being sent out to the fleet, many of us recruits going overseas for the first time. The strictest seniority is the navy's operating rule, and what this means in practical terms is that all the menial jobs that have to be done every day to keep things running fall to the newest and the lowliest in rank. My introduction to this rule came at once and in the classic way—as "captain of the head." The moment I stepped aboard, I was assigned to keep spotless and shined to a high gloss the decks, the showers, the basins, and the troughs of running seawater in several heads. I craned my neck out of a porthole to see Point Loma, the dangling peninsula that protected San Diego harbor, known to generations of sailors as "Point Hard-On" because of its shape and its effect on those returning from—not going on—long voyages overseas. Once around Point Loma and into blue water the ship began to pick up speed, and as she did, she began to pitch and roll. My stomach, never having been at sea before, heaved for a while and then groaned for a day or two while I swung the heavy swab to clean the head until my appetite came back and my sea legs set. I was never seasick again in my life.

Five days out we came in the early morning around Diamond Head and went down the shore opposite Honolulu and then through the nets and buoys into the narrow entrance to Pearl Harbor. The water formed a ring around Ford Island, the pearl in the center of the anchorage, the naval air station where the patrol squadrons of PBYs, the Catalina flying boats, were based and where the squadrons from the aircraft carriers operated while they were in port. The *Procyon* tied up in the navy yard, and immediately a swarm of motor whaleboats arrived to pick up the personnel assigned to the various ships and deliver them to their new homes. The air was electric: the tropical surroundings and soft smells, the huge and busy naval base, the ships of all kinds—battleships, aircraft carriers, submarines, cruisers, destroyers, minesweepers. If you were of a warlike turn of mind, this was the place, fairly breathing the invincible power of the United States Navy.

Still eager to work with airplanes, I considered it a stroke of good luck that I had been assigned to Torpedo Squadron 6, part of the air group on the USS *Enterprise* (CV-6), one of three carriers in the Pacific Fleet at that time, along with the older *Lexington* and *Saratoga*. The sister ship of the *Enterprise,* the USS *Yorktown* (CV-5), was on her way to the Pacific. The *Enterprise* was tied up on the western side of Ford Island taking on supplies, and as the motor whaleboat came up under her counter on her seaward, port, side, she towered a hundred feet above us, grayish white, nearly nine hundred feet long, beautifully proportioned despite her size. The squadron was in barracks ashore with the planes, but I was assigned a bunk on ship and given an hour to wander around, staring with wonder at the complicated machinery, elevators, and spare planes tied up in the overhead of the vast hangar deck. It was all very busy, the sailors—a crew of two thousand—in spotless white shorts and T-shirts rushing here and there, the public-address system constantly blaring out bugle calls, the shrill of the boatswain's whistles, and unintelligible orders to "hear this" or "hear that," or that sounded something like, "Flemish down the bosun's lines." Mine was a total and instant love affair with this great ship, never lost and never experienced again in quite the same way with another.

The *Enterprise* became the most famous of American warships, in all wars. She was in eighteen major actions, hit by bombs many times but never by a torpedo; she downed 911 enemy planes with her guns and planes. Her planes sank 71 enemy ships and damaged or destroyed 192 more. When she was about to be broken up for scrap after the war, there was a national campaign to raise money to save her as a museum. I thought about it but decided not to contribute because I didn't want to think of her sitting around in some backwater, being exploited in unworthy ways. Better by far, I thought, to leave her to the memory of those who had served on her when she was fully alive, vibrating under full steam at thirty-two knots, the aircraft turning up, guns firing, heeling over so sharply that the hangar deck took on water to avoid the bombs. Others must have felt the same way, for the funds fell short, and having gone through nearly every major engagement on the long road to Tokyo, she was broken up for scrap. Better that, I still think, than to be like the *Intrepid* in New York Harbor, where the school groups clatter and squeal, the professional veterans come to be photographed, and the politicians make patriotic speeches on holidays.

I was brought down to earth that afternoon by being put on the anchor chain work detail. Life on board ship is a constant battle with rust, in which the weapons are the chipping hammer, the wire brush, red lead, and gray paint. The anchor chain is always rusty and while in port is regularly taken out of the chain storage and laid out in a barge alongside the ship, each huge link more than three feet in length. The trick is to chip off all the old paint, wire brush the rust off down to bare pitted metal, and put on a priming coat of red lead followed by two or three coats of navy dark gray paint. Hard work, dirty, tiring, hot, and totally unrewarded unless by knowing that you had done a good job. The members of the air group, called Airedales by the rest of the crew, were normally exempt from this kind of ship's work, but the real king of the ship, Jocko—a boatswain's mate first class, the ship's master-at-arms, a kind of chief of police-cum-ward politician—was happy to hold transfers like me in his transit group as long as possible to supply manpower for such jobs.

After a few days the ground crews of the air group came back aboard in preparation for sailing, and Murphy, the chief of the ordnance gang in the torpedo squadron, instantly reclaimed me on the usual grounds that he was already shorthanded and needed every trained man he could get. The deck crews regarded this as bushwa, just a plausible Airedale excuse, but the ship officially recognized the airplanes as her primary armament and gave priority to their operation. I was overjoyed to be given a bunk in the squadron compartment, made known to the leading chief and the yeomen who kept the records, and, above all, given a place, however low, in the ordnance gang, which meant a coffee cup and the right to sit around in the ordnance shack, a wire-mesh enclosure suspended just below the flight deck where tools were kept. Here Murphy and his leading petty officer, Freddy Moyle, a refugee from the British navy, kept court, quietly and happily buzzed all day long on "moosemilk," a mixture of coffee and bombsight alcohol of 99 percent purity used for cleaning the Norden bombsights, the supply of which was fortuitously in Murph's charge.

Ordnancemen worked in pairs: an experienced petty officer and a striker, the navy's name for an apprentice, like me, learning the ropes. Each pair was responsible for three planes, seeing to it that the guns were kept clean and adjusted, the bomb racks working, the torpedo gear ready to go when needed, and so on. Much of the work was more communal, involving the whole ordnance gang: belting ammunition, bringing bombs up from the magazine and fusing them, hauling the torpedoes out on long hydraulic trucks to the planes and loading them, changing bomb racks so that different weights of bombs could be carried. It required a lot of running about and a lot of savvy, which came only with practice.

The torpedo squadron of eighteen planes at full complement, which was seldom, was one of four making up the air group. Besides the "fish" there were two identical squadrons of eighteen dive-bombers, one specializing in scouting (VS-6), and one in dive-bombing (VB-6). Providing cover for the ship and protection for the torpedo planes and bombers was a squadron of eighteen fighter planes (VF-6). Together these seventy-two planes were judged able to deliver a deadly coordinated attack against any naval target, the fighters flying protection overhead, the dive-bombers going in first from high altitude, followed at sea level by the torpedo planes to deliver the coup to the enemy ships. To me, with my limited conceptions of warfare, it all looked like the most up-to-date and modern technology, Buck Rogers himself. The officers who flew in the squadrons and ran the ships were as naive about their equipment and tactics as I was.

The torpedo plane came from the mid-thirties. The TBD-1, translated "torpedo bomber, made by Douglas Aircraft, model 1," was obsolete. Designed to carry three men—pilot, observer-bomber in the center, and radioman gunner in the rear—it could do only about a hundred knots with a torpedo, a fatally slow speed for escaping shipboard antiaircraft gunners and fast fighter planes. It was not much faster with a load of two five-hundred-pound bombs, or eight one-hundred-pounders, and used with these bomb loads as a high-level bomber with the Norden bombsight it was long out of date. Its armament was extremely modest: one .30-caliber fixed machine gun synchronized to fire forward through the propeller and one free .30 caliber in the rear fired by the radioman. Later there were two guns in the rear, but the increase in fire power was offset by the awkwardness of handling their weight in the slipstream. About all you could say in praise of the old "Devastator," as it was styled, was that with its huge wingspan, it seldom crashed, and it floated onto the deck at a nice slow landing speed. But to me it looked like some spaceship ready for Mars, and I polished up all the ordnance gear on my planes daily, disassembled the guns down to the smallest parts, cleaned them, and adjusted the headspace far more often than was needed.

The dive-bomber, the SBD Douglas "Dauntless," was the top of the line and would become the primary naval aircraft during the first two years of the war. The fighter plane, the F4F-3, the Grumman "Wildcat," was new and powerful but definitely inferior to the Japanese fighter, the Zero, that would be its primary opponent in 1942 at the Coral Sea, Midway, and the Solomons.

The demand for labor of the most basic kind was endless on board ship, and a sailor's first year or two in the fleet was usually spent going from one kind of scut work to another. As the lowest in the squadron pecking order, I was soon off to the plane-handling crews, a life that was healthy but exhausting. My days from before dawn until after dark were spent on the flight deck, wearing a dark blue T-shirt and a canvas helmet dyed the same color buckled tightly under the chin, pushing planes at a dead run back and forth on the flight deck and the hangar deck. There was barely enough room on the two decks for all the planes after space was left for landing or taking off, and they had to be spotted with the greatest skill, like the puzzles with moveable pieces and only one empty space. When planes were about to land, all the planes on the flight deck had to be pushed forward to leave enough room aft. Those for which there was no space were pushed onto one of the three elevators and taken down to the hangar deck, where other crews picked them up and moved them around that deck. When planes were taking off, the process was reversed, with all the planes to be launched spotted aft on the flight deck with clear space in front of them. Then, as the ship turned into the wind and went to high speed to provide the greatest possible wind speed over the deck, the plane taking off went to full power with the brakes on, released them suddenly, and used the combination of its forward speed and the wind to lift it (usually) into the air by the time it reached the forward end of the deck.

As soon as the planes were off, the blue plane handlers leaped out of the catwalks alongside the flight deck, where we had been waiting, and began to re-spot the deck for the next planes coming in to land. In the days before tractors were used to pull the planes, all of this complicated maneuvering was done entirely by man power. Since the battle effectiveness of the carrier depended on the speed and efficiency with which it moved its planes for launching and landing, keeping the deck as prepared as possible to launch an attack, this was a high-pressure business, with a lot of shouting and running all day long, a lot like athletic teams. Except for lunch, you never left the deck from the time flight operations began, before light, until they ended, after dark, and any moment of rest was passed sitting at the side of the island, asleep in an instant, so that you could be there immediately if needed. Lots of military drills are more show than reality, but this one was in dead earnest, timed with a stopwatch. In the coming war, battles were lost and won by the plane-handling on the carriers. The Japanese lost the Battle of Midway in large part because of a systematic failure to handle their planes properly.

The *Enterprise* left Pearl Harbor at the end of November, loaded with, in addition to her own air group, the fighter planes of a marine squadron that was to be taken to Wake Island and flown off to the landing strip there. Wake was the closest of our bases to Japan, and the faces of the pilots were grim when they flew off to the island. In a few weeks they had all been captured or killed, including a boy named Bobby Mitwalsky, who had gone to school with me and joined the marines when I went into the navy. I remembered him most for a leather jacket he had with panels of admirable blue fur.

The clouds were heavy all the way back from Wake and the storms continuous, waves breaking over the flight deck when the bow dipped deep. The other ships in the task force, cruisers and destroyers, began to make heavy going of it, and the task force slowed down, delaying its entrance into Pearl Harbor from the night of December 6 to sometime in the morning of the 7th.

Whenever the *Enterprise* went into port, because she could not launch or land aircraft while tied up, the planes were flown off to a land base for as long as we were in harbor. Early on the morning of the 7th our air group took off for Ford Island. The ship was empty, without its planes, and everyone was getting ready for docking in Berth 1010 alongside the navy yard and the starboard watch going ashore for liberty. But before 0900 hours, general quarters was sounded—a clanging bell followed by a boatswain's pipe and a stirring bugle call. A stern voice ordered, "All hands man your battle stations," at the sound of which all hell broke loose, and thousands of sailors ran to their assigned battle stations. You had to race up ladders and down passageways to get through before all watertight doors and hatches were closed and dogged down. No one was surprised—submarine scares were common—but this was different. A huge battle flag was broken out and streamed down the deck. The captain came on the public address system to announce that Pearl Harbor had been bombed and that we were now at war with the Japanese. This was followed by the reading of the Articles of War, a long list, I thought, of the many reasons for which the navy could imprison you for life or shoot you. It spoke of no rewards.

I didn't worry about being killed, but I did wonder how long I was going to have to stay in the navy now. We all disliked the Japanese and the Germans in a general kind of way, not really knowing much about them. But I never saw a newspaper, only the daily mimeographed sheet put out aboard ship with ball scores and a few headlines, and I knew nothing of how oil embargoes and blocked finances had brought us to war. I knew that the Japanese had invaded China long ago and were still fighting there. Everyone knew the Japanese hated us, even as we despised them, and the old Asiatic hands told stories of Japanese sailors lining up at the rail and shouting, "Yankee, we sink you," when they passed in port. So, really, it was no surprise, somehow expected and taken for granted for a long time, though the reasons were beyond us.

The ship stayed at general quarters; we were only a few miles south of the entrance to Pearl Harbor, and the scuttlebutt (named after the water cask on the old ships where sailors getting a drink of water exchanged gossip) began to circulate that the Japanese had landed on Oahu, taken San Francisco, and on and on. Rumor is a remarkable thing, a free play of the imagination, but the truth was that after two air strikes the Japanese planes went back to their carriers north of Oahu, which turned at high speed and went back to their home ports. We looked for the Japanese fleet in an unlikely direction, southwest, and fortunately never found it, for although some of our planes had returned to the ship—others had gotten mixed up in the battle and been shot down—a single carrier with few planes aboard would have been no match for the enemy's six carriers.

Fuel was low in all the ships in the task force, and we had to go into port in the late afternoon of December 8, fueling that night and putting to sea by dawn. Rumors of new attacks were everywhere, and since no one knew where the attack had come from, there was fear that it might come again. Everyone was keyed up and the ship remained at general quarters, which meant that I was on the flight deck, where I could see everything in the fading light. The smells came first as we moved slowly through the nets guarding the channel, smells of fuel oil, burned paint and canvas, hot steel. Fires were still burning, and a heavy cloud of smoke hung over ships that had looked so bright a week earlier. It was eerie, the huge ship moving painstakingly slowly into the harbor through what had always been a narrow channel, now made now much narrower by a battleship half in the mud on the port side, its stern sticking well out into the channel. The *Nevada* had managed to get under way during the attack but began to founder going out of the channel. The captain, realizing that if his ship sank in the channel it would block the Pacific Fleet from entering or exiting, beached her on the western side, leaving just enough room for the big carrier and her escorts to maneuver around him at painfully slow speed.

After inching around the *Nevada*—oh, how slow it was when all we wanted to do was get it over with and get out of there—the *Enterprise* turned a few points to port and started down the anchorage between battleship row to port and the dockyard and submarine base to starboard. At the naval yard, aft of a huge drydock containing the battleship *Pennsylvania,* were the cruiser *Helena* and the minesweeper *Oglala.* Japanese intelligence had predicted that the aircraft carrier *Enterprise* would be in this position on December 7, and a torpedo intended for her smashed into the smaller ships. The entire front of the navy yard, including the immense drydock with the *Pennsylvania* inside, accompanied by a badly hit destroyer, was blasted and strewn with rubble of broken ships and installations. But for some reason the Japanese had neglected to bomb the all-important fuel storage tanks on the hill beyond the yard. The operation of the fleet depended on this fuel.

It was on the port side, however, that the real devastation was visible, beginning with wrecked hangars and seaplanes on the tip of Ford Island, then, one after another—broken in two, turned over, canted crazily, lying under water with only the upper masts showing, burned, smoking, and smoldering—the long row of battleships, two by two, the main battle force of the Pacific Fleet and the U.S. Navy. The attack announced in a violent way that the day of the battleship was gone, that it had been replaced by aircraft carriers like the one that was now picking her way daintily, almost disdainfully, down the harbor past the smoking hulks of the old navy devastated by planes from foreign aircraft carriers.

The meaning extended even further, for the carrier-based Japanese planes not only sank the American battleships they sank at the same time all the huge battleships that the Japanese Imperial Navy had been building for many years. The Japanese would emphasize the lesson on the other side of the Pacific Ocean when off Malaya they sank the British battleships *Prince of Wales* and *Repulse* with land-based torpedo aircraft as the ships were under way and combat ready, not tied up. Having seen the mighty effects of air power, I was stunned, and more than a little frightened, by this sudden destruction of what had seemed invincible a week earlier. There was no question of losing the war, but how would we win it? Surely not with a few aircraft carriers like the *Enterprise,* but there wasn't anything else.

One dreary scene succeeded another, and as night fell we inched in slow motion around the northern end of Ford Island, like some skulking mourner at a ghastly funeral. Loud voices called out from shore: "You'd better get the hell out of here or the Japs will get you too." And "Where in hell were you?" A few guns went off here and there, and machine-gun tracers rose in the air from time to time as nervous gunners let loose at their fears and confusion. Then, to port, we passed the old target battleship *Utah,* with her bottom turned up to the sky, and we tied up just beyond her. The fuel lines came aboard in an instant, and all hands that could be spared from battle stations, which included me, formed lines down the gangways onto Ford Island to pass the supplies that were waiting there for us into the ship.

Each sailor was given postcards to send home: two with the printed message "I am well and will write soon," another two with "I am wounded and will write details as soon as possible." We joked that there should be a third message, "I am dead." Laughter aside, at this point a fatal train was lighted that would explode months later in my family's mountain ranch. Two cards meant one for the family and one for the girlfriend all sailors claimed to have. I did not have a girlfriend, wasn't even sure I wanted one, but you had to live up to the heroic moment, which required a girlfriend, so I sent my second card off to a girl in Saratoga whom I much admired but who was indifferent to me. The cards became separated in transit, and the card to the girl arrived first, while the one to my family was delayed. The ranch was snowed in, but someone trudged the four miles through the snow to tell my parents that Jane had heard from me and I was safe. My mother was relieved, but, suffering already from depression, which had been intensified by my going overseas and the beginning of the war, she concluded that I no longer cared for her and had transferred my loyalties to a girl she didn't like. She assumed that I had had only one card and had used it to write to Jane, and when her card arrived a week or two later, it made no difference to her feelings about my disloyalty.

By three or four in the morning the ship was loaded, many of the supplies still on the hangar deck waiting to be stowed below. The lines were cast off, and the *Enterprise* began to edge her way out the harbor, down the channel, through the nets, and into blue water, picking up speed as she went, the sun rising, the water beginning to hiss alongside, and the smell of oil, charred paint, bodies, and defeat left far behind. Our air group landed aboard later, and the war had begun.

FOUR

Cruising

To a young man war is exciting, and few wars can have looked more promising at the beginning than the naval war in the Pacific Ocean between the United States and Japan from December 1941 to September 1945. The ocean itself was vast and filled with mysterious places whose exotic names now became as familiar to me as the little towns in Wyoming where I had grown up—Medicine Bow, Rawlins, Encampment, and Laramie—once had been. Now the names were Truk (the major Japanese base in the Marianas Islands), Cavite and Bataan, the Java Sea and the Coral Sea, Guam and Wake Island, Mindanao and Balikpapan, New Caledonia and Guadalcanal.

Great fleets steamed across vast spaces of water at high speed, surprising the enemy with sudden raids and then disappearing into the emptiness extending from the Aleutians and the Bering Strait in the north to Port Moresby and New Zealand in the south, from the California coast to the Indian Ocean. The ships were fast, heavily armed, and technically advanced; never before tried in combat, they were now about to develop by trial and error a new kind of war of aircraft carriers: ship-based aircraft fighting with other ship-based aircraft for control of the air and sea.

The crews on both sides at that early point in the war were professional and volunteer; everyone was there because he had wanted, or at least agreed, to be there, and as a consequence the morale was high, as were the skills of the combatants. It was a war both navies had wanted for a long time, and, tired of messing with each other, they went at it with a lot of energy. We despised the Japanese at first, and it took a lot of failures to realize that at the beginning of the war theirs was a better navy than ours: better aircraft, better trained personnel, better night training, better torpedoes by far. We improved rapidly, but in the end we overcame them by sheer weight of equipment and men. They remained to the end a worthy foe—courageous, skilled, tenacious, gallant in their strange way—whom we had seriously underestimated. Never after the first days of the war did the sailors in our fleet look down on "the Japs" or speak contemptuously, like our yellow press, of the cowardice of the enemy.

Most of us on the *Enterprise* assumed after Pearl Harbor that the ship and the other carriers in the Pacific would be sent at once to relieve the Philippines and to break up the attack on Wake Island. Our admiral, William F. "Bull" Halsey, a real fire-eater, thought so too. His quarters were just down the passageway, beneath the flight deck and the island, from our ordnance shack, and when we went down to try to wheedle fresh fruit from his mess attendants we could hear him thundering away, cursing Washington and the shore-based navy for their cowardice. The only reason we could think of for not being sent to sink the Japanese fleet forthwith—this is how we thought in our innocence—was that nearly all our battleships were lying broken and burned on the mud bottom of the anchorages alongside Ford Island. But Adm. Chester Nimitz, soon to be the commander of the Pacific Fleet, must have had some understanding of what Pearl Harbor meant for the long run, for later, when he was assembling the fleet to fight the Battle of Midway, he left out several seaworthy battleships that were assembled in San Francisco.

Wisely, no one ordered us to fight our way to Manila, Truk, or Yokosuka, and we were kept on patrols during December and early January, guarding the approaches to the Hawaiian Islands, going back and forth across the 180th meridian, the International Date Line. On December 24, 1941, with a satisfactory kind of black humor, we crossed the dateline to the west at midnight, going straight to December 26, never missing Noel and God Rest You Merry Gentlemen.

The American carriers—there were only three, *Lexington, Yorktown,* and *Enterprise,* after the *Saratoga* was hit by a torpedo in early January— operated separately, each the center of a task force completed by heavy cruisers and destroyers. Standard watches were Condition Three (four hours on duty and eight off) and Condition Two (four hours on and four off), with most watertight doors and hatches dogged closed. It was difficult to move about the ship, and everyone was always tired. Reveille came before sunrise so that general quarters could be sounded in time for everyone to be at their battle stations at sunrise. Sunrise and sunset were considered the two most dangerous moments, when submarine or airplane attacks could be made out of the sun. Six fighter planes would be launched just before sunup to fly combat air patrol (CAP) over the task force, and soon after a number of dive-bombers and torpedo planes armed with aerial depth charges would be sent up to fly searches out a hundred miles (ASP) or more looking for submarines or surface vessels. After the planes were off the deck and general quarters secured, the smoking lamp was lit, and breakfast was served. Coffee and beans, sometimes Spam, occasionally dried eggs, dry cereal with powdered milk, prunes, or some other kind of dried or canned fruit. Oranges or apples if you had been in port recently. Then the day's work began, cleaning and polishing, repairing the equipment for which you were responsible, belting ammunition, providing working parties for one job after another, and the dreaded chipping detail. Peacetime navy ships were beautifully painted inside and out, and the lower decks were covered with thick red linoleum kept at a high shine. The Pearl Harbor attack, however, had shown that paint and linoleum burn fiercely, giving off a heavy toxic smoke, and so after December 7 ships were ordered to get rid of all the interior paint, except in the light-green officers' quarters, and all the linoleum.

The interior of a carrier, like that of other warships, is a maze of hatches, welded supports, air ducts, cables, and pipes, all covered generously with several coats of white paint, and to chip it all off, flake by flake, with a chipping hammer—a flat iron bar, bent at a right angle two inches from one end, and sharpened on both ends—was a labor of the damned. It was hot inside the ship, and the men stripped to their skivvies, rags around their heads, chipping away—clink, clink, clink, sonofabitch!—hour after hour. It was maddening work, difficult, endless, seemingly pointless, and when it was finished, after many months in which it took up every spare hour, and the linoleum ripped off the rusty decks, the compartments with their raw, rust-pitted bulkheads were as depressing as if the ship had been burned out.

Watching the task force spread out over the ocean never ceased to be interesting, even after months of steaming. The carrier was in the center, and the cruisers *Salt Lake City, Northampton, Chester,* and *Pensacola* plunged steadily along on both sides. Ten or twelve destroyers raced about on the flanks, ahead, and to the stern, listening for submarines, transferring material and personnel, and serving as plane guards to pick up the crews of crashed planes.

We refueled at sea, and occasionally a big tanker named after a faraway American river—the Platte or the Cimarron—would come alongside, some fifty feet away, and with both ships still under way, pitching and rolling toward each other, these thousands of tons of mass would send rubber hoses across and pump fuel and aviation gas out of the tanker into the carrier. Sometimes, as we became more adept, a cruiser or destroyer would get fuel at the same time on the other side of the tanker, or would take fuel from the carrier herself on the side away from the tanker. During this operation the waves between the ships were huge, and standing on the deck of the carrier you could watch the great bulk of the tanker rise up above you and then crash down. It was blue-water seamanship at its best, always pleasant to watch how smartly it was done. It permitted our ships to stay at sea much longer and to operate while there without having to run at slow speeds to conserve fuel. It also meant that, keeping radio silence, you could disappear in the distances of the ocean, to appear suddenly somewhere you weren't expected or wanted.

At the beginning of February 1942, the *Enterprise,* on the first major American carrier raid of the war, appeared out of the blue in this way to attack Kwajalein Atoll in the Marshall Islands. We had been down to Samoa escorting troop ships and looking longingly at the green tropical islands off in the far distance. The *Yorktown* had come around from the Atlantic, and after we joined her, we had moved north together. The run in to the islands began at high speed in the evening and continued all night long. For the first time, we sweated through the night before the battle. The crew's compartments were aft, where, lying in your bunk with the whole stern of the ship vibrating from the propeller shafts turning at high rpms below, sleep was fitful. There was a general uneasiness, which the crew, restless with the noise and rattle, the shush of the air ducts bringing fresh air to compartments in which all portholes had been covered, communicated by endless nervous shifting in the bunks and constant movement back and forth to the heads in the red glare of the nightlights. During battle conditions the red lights went out, and the blue battle lamps here and there created an eerie, never-to-be-forgotten spooky feeling, as the sweat dripped down into your eyes from under your gray steel World War I helmet, the stale camphor smell of the fireproofed canvas covers of the bulky gray kapok-filled life jackets tied tightly up under your chin.

Reveille was a relief. We rushed to get up to the deck, hoping to see the islands we were attacking, but there were only the familiar blue water and the escort vessels. Kwajalein Atoll was still many miles away, attacked but never seen by the carrier's crew. The strike force—a few torpedo planes carrying bombs for a high-level attack, some dive-bombers each carrying a yellow five-hundred-pound bomb under the fuselage, and a handful of fighters to provide air cover—went off about 0500, and the cruisers moved in to shell the landing fields. At that time it seemed a mighty air armada to us, who had not yet seen the sky filled from horizon to horizon with carrier planes on their way to the Japanese mainland. I was released from plane-pushing duties to help load bombs onto the torpedo planes, hoisting them up and locking them on the bomb rack, inserting the fuses and threading the long copper arming wire through the holes in the fuse vanes, tightening up the sway brackets.

Off in the distance the strike group was no bigger than a fist held up in the sky, and the *Enterprise* was still with her planes gone. Everyone waited nervously to see whether we had been spotted by the enemy. Ship's radar was primitive in those days, but we did have it, and the Japanese did not—one of our few advantages—and this morning it kept telling us that the skies were clear. The Japanese planes had been caught on the ground with their ships in the anchorage inside the big atoll. Then the wait began for the return of our own planes, and about mid-morning a few fighters came back, then some dive-bombers, and at last the torpedo planes. All eyes tried to count to see how many planes had been lost. Only a few, it turned out, not more than three or four.

The *Enterprise* turned into the wind, picked up maximum speed, cleared the flight deck, and raised the arresting cables to catch the planes' tailhooks. The hydraulic crash barriers three-quarters of the way up the deck came up with a swoosh, and the carrier was ready to take her strike group aboard. The planes roared by in loose formation on the starboard side, a few hundred feet up, and as they passed the ship, they began to peel off, one by one, to their port, flying around the ship and coming in low and aft, following the wake onto the deck. The landing signal officer stood at the rear on the port side, facing aft, with two yellow paddles, one in each hand, giving visual signals to the incoming plane. Up a little, a bit to port, less power, cut.

The plane hit the deck heavily, and its hook grabbed one of the elevated arresting wires and jerked it out until the plane came to a stop. Men raced out to release the arresting wire, the tailhook retracted, the crash barriers went down, the plane taxied forward at high speed, then slammed on the brakes, and the barrier came back up just as the next plane was landing. It was a tricky and a dangerous business, and everything depended on doing it fast and doing it well. In peacetime the navy was miserly about every piece of equipment, but in wartime a badly damaged plane went over the side instantly to clear room for the following plane.

How effective the strike had been no one seemed to know, and if they did, no one bothered to tell the crew, who filled what later times would call an information gap with scuttlebutt about monstrous battle-ships sinking in the channel, hundreds of planes exploding from direct hits while taxiing out to take off, and disgraced and distraught Japanese admirals committing hara-kiri in the control tower to apologize to the emperor. Quite satisfying stuff, which made the morning seem extremely worthwhile, though in fact the few planes with their light bomb loads had done little harm.

After a small follow-up strike was launched, we were told to rearm all the torpedo planes with torpedoes, which were considered, as the Japanese had demonstrated at Pearl Harbor, the right weapons with which to sink warships. Quick, an older ordnanceman, and I were moving one of the stubby two-thousand-pound aerial torpedoes on a hydraulic lift across the oily, slippery hangar deck. Suddenly the five-inch antiaircraft guns on the after starboard sponson above began firing, and the deck heeled sharply up fifteen degrees on that side as the ship turned abruptly to port to evade an attack. The PA blared, STAND BY TO REPEL ENEMY AIR ATTACK. My first immediate experience of a shooting war! A big Japanese patrol plane had found us. The steep angle of the deck caused the heavy torpedo to slide down toward the port side, carrying us with it. We lowered the hydraulic skid to the deck, but it continued sliding on the oily steel until secured to a ring in the deck used for tying down planes. There we stood, frozen, two sailors with a lashed-down torpedo, in the middle of the vast, empty hangar deck, which was shifting rapidly from one crazy angle to another. I wanted to get the hell out of there, but we couldn't leave the torpedo for fear it would break loose and smash into a bulkhead and explode. The progress of the attack could be measured, even when you couldn't see anything, by the number and caliber of guns firing. As long as only the five-inchers were booming, the enemy was still high and far away, but when the small-caliber guns cut in (first the four-barreled, deliberate one-point-ones—bang, bang, bang, bang—and then the .50-caliber machine guns along the catwalks), it was time to put your head down. When someone ran out on the deck and began firing a hand-gun, which occasionally happened, the attack was really closing in. After the fifties cut in water splashed in one of the openings of the hangar deck from a near miss. In a few minutes it was all over.

The *Enterprise,* undamaged, was on her way back to Pearl Harbor one bright blue day when one of our torpedo planes flying a search vector failed to return. We waited for it and the three men aboard for hours until we were certain that it must have run out of gas in an area where there was no place to land except on the deck of the *Enterprise.* Search planes went out, and destroyers patrolled for miles in all directions, but no trace of the plane was found, and the men were assumed lost. When they turned up in Pearl Harbor about two months later, we were all astounded. They had spent thirty days on their small yellow rubber raft, all three of them, with no rations or water, having lost everything when they ditched. Rainwater, seabirds, and fish kept them going until, purely by chance in all that vast-ness, they washed ashore on a small island, losing their raft getting across the coral reef.

The March 23, 1942, issue of *Time* magazine referred to the pilot, an enlisted chief aviation pilot named Harold Dixon, as "a man that Bligh would fancy," and encouraged by this double-edged praise, he published a book, *The Raft,* with the aid of a ghostwriter who made him quite a hero. The writer had him saying, for example, when his crew lay exhausted, emaciated, and dehydrated on the beach of the island, "If there are Japs on this island, they'll not see an American sailor crawl. We'll stand like men-of-warsmen." Everyone hooted at this, and the squadron wits did some very funny acts standing like "men-of-warsmen," a role no one had heard of for years. Tony Pastula, the middle-seat man, told us that Dixon had failed to make a crucial turn on the patrol, and when the radioman, Aldrich, told him that the ship's homing signal was getting weaker, Dixon told him to shut up, that he had been flying by the seat of his pants longer than Aldrich had been a radioman. In the end they ran out of gas and took to their raft, and after Aldrich, not Dixon, dragged them out of the surf, they were saved by the natives and some nuns. The raft went into the U.S. Naval Academy Museum, where it is still displayed, and the book made a lot of money, but the ghostwriter and Dixon cut Pastula and Aldrich out of the deal. Tony said that they had been conned into signing a paper to surrender their rights to the story in return for five hundred dollars each. But at least they became members of the "Sea Squatters," a club organized by Kidde, the company that made the small CO_2 bottles that inflated the navy rafts and Mae Wests.

Entering Pearl Harbor after the Marshall raid may have been the most moving moment of the war for me, far more than seeing Nagasaki, which was hard to take in, or Tokyo Bay, which was anticlimactic. We were in whites, lined up at quarters on the flight deck, and as we came down the channel, the sunken and burned battleships in plain sight along Ford Island, the crews of the anchored ships, at quarters themselves, their white uniforms showing up against their gray ships, cheered us, one after another, again and again. The frustration of defeat and helplessness after

Pearl Harbor, while the Japanese overran the entire western Pacific and sank our ships wherever they found them, in the Philippines and Indonesia, was enormous. The raid on the Marshalls, followed by other raids on small islands like Wake and Marcus, was the first successful action by an American ship; small, yes, but it was enough to give the fleet a lift.

The feeling of being a hero didn't last long. I had already been a plane handler, but that was a noble occupation compared to mess cooking: three months in the galleys, literally, peeling potatoes in enormous machines, washing huge pots and pans, serving food to endless lines of sailors making nasty remarks about what you gave them. Mess cooking was exile. You had to move to the mess halls with your sea bag, stow your hammock in the nets there, and sleep in it at night, one of the few places in the navy where hammocks were still used. The food-serving operation ran night and day, with watches coming on and going off duty every four hours, and only the exhaustion after long days of heavy labor made sleep possible in compartments where the lights were never out and noisy people came and went constantly.

One of the most disagreeable jobs was handling the huge galvanized garbage cans filled to the brim with slops to be dumped over the side. It took two men to get them up the slippery, narrow ship's ladders, step by painful step, with some inevitable spillage, to where they could be emptied over the side, to leeward, of course, which was not always an easy place to find in the dark if the ship was maneuvering and the wind was shifting. The job was made more difficult by the fact that it had to be done after darken ship to avoid showing a trail in the ocean until the fish had a chance to clean up after us. One night my fellow garbage handler, Whitey, and I fell on a steep ladder. In a failed attempt to keep the can from spilling, Whitey slipped and hit his mouth on the edge of the can, knocking out one of his upper front teeth. The ship's dentist did only fillings and extractions, no cosmetic work, and so Whitey spent his next few liberties—we got liberty only every month or two when we came into

Pearl—going to a Honolulu dentist to get a false tooth. This was both a joyless and expensive way to spend what little liberty and money he had, even though by that time we were seamen first class, making all of fifty-four dollars a month, and I used to argue with him long and earnestly, in the way that only a young man who knows nothing about the matter could, that it was pointless to waste his time and money in this fashion. Better to wait until the war was over and you knew whether you would survive to use a false tooth, ran my foolish and boring refrain.

But Whitey was not only stubborn, he was, it turned out to my vast surprise, hugely vain, and though small and nondescript physically, like the rest of us—we did not look at all like the sailors we occasionally saw gaily dancing their lives away in movie musicals!—he could not bear the thought of being what he considered mutilated. He was right, I suppose, but there was something to be said for my perception. After he became an apprentice cook Whitey was killed by an armor-piercing bomb that exploded in the *Enterprise*'s chiefs' galley the following October at the Battle of Santa Cruz.

Honolulu in those days, where we took our brief, eight-hour liberties, was more out of Somerset Maugham than Gauguin, but it seemed a proper setting for the old salts we thought we were by that time. Dressed in fresh white uniforms, we rushed onto the buses and roared down to Canal Street. A few minutes were spent in the New Congress Hotel where the "French line" went up the long wooden stairs on the right, and the "old-fashioned" line ascended the left staircase. Such sophistication! Going through both lines—take your choice of the order—was considered a sign of super manhood. Weaker spirits were likely to wander off to have a few beers before going through the line, but older hands knew from experience that the unspeakable local brew, Primo Beer, which was loaded with saltpeter—at least so it was said—would douse the flames of lust faster than a fire hose.

I fancied myself quite a dancer at the time, and I found my way in time to the servicemen's club—the USO that had just been opened—to dance with the local Portuguese girls who volunteered to mingle with the sailors. Honolulu was an old liberty port, long familiar with naval antics ashore, and while nothing we did could any longer surprise the outrage-hardened citizenry, they wanted as little to do with us as possible. In particular, they did not want us even to look at their daughters. Unaware of the reputation of sailors in Honolulu, though, I thought I cut quite a fine nautical figure and was crestfallen when I tried to make a date with a beautiful Portuguese girl, only to learn that her father would rather see her date one of the lepers from Molokai than a sailor. But my heart was not broken.

On to the honky-tonks with the jukeboxes, the fights between sailors from different ships, and several bottles of the abominable Primo, no hard liquor being sold. Dirty, bedraggled, and obscenely noisy, we made our way back to the navy yard by late afternoon, ran the gauntlet of the marine guards at the gate who took out their frustrations, with clubs, on sailors looking for a fight, and then crowded into the fifty-foot motor launches that took us at last back to ships with names as epic—*Enterprise, Yorktown, Salt Lake City, Northampton*—as those at Trafalgar or Jutland. Weighed soberly, Honolulu liberty was not much, but it had the effect of making us glad to be, as sailors always are, aboard ship and at sea again.

In April we put to sea and to our surprise went north for a change. Morale dropped with the news that Bataan had surrendered. As it became cold and colder, woolen watch caps and winter uniforms, long stowed away in storage lockers, appeared. White water broke over the flight deck as the ship rose and fell in heavy seas. One morning there was another carrier, the USS *Hornet* (CV-8), younger sister ship of the *Enterprise,* running alongside us, about a hundred yards away. Instead of the usual pale-blue-and-white naval aircraft, her deck was loaded with twin-engine army bombers, Mitchell B-25s, from a point forward of the island all the way to the stern. We assumed that they were intended for delivery somewhere in the Aleutians, but the public address system soon announced (there was no need for secrecy since there was no one we could tell and no way we could tell them) that this was an army squadron commanded by Col. James Doolittle, to be launched for an attack on Tokyo after we took it to a point five hundred miles off the Japanese mainland. The *Enterprise* was to provide combat air patrols and antisubmarine patrols for the *Hornet* since she could launch none of her own planes while the Mitchells filled her flight deck.

We were excited not only at the idea of hitting Tokyo itself but also at the danger of going so close to Japan. But we were technicians, and it was the technical problem that really intrigued us. Could the heavy planes with a bomb load of four five-hundred-pounders, even when stripped of guns and armor, get to Japan and then make it to the nearest safe landing point in China? Even before that, could such heavy planes, designed for long airfields, get off a short carrier deck? The B-25s spotted farthest forward had a run of only about three hundred feet, which was about the minimum run needed for even the much smaller carrier planes designed for this work. Sailors, like stockbrokers, work everything out by betting, and there was soon heavy money down on both sides: would they make it, would they not? The odds were that the B-25s wouldn't have been on the *Hornet* if there had not been successful tests somewhere, but with all the skepticism of an old salt about anything the services did, I put down ten dollars at even money that less than half of them would get into the air.

April 18 was a cold and windy morning: near gale-force winds with high green foam-flecked waves and the taste and smell of the northern ocean. We were spotted some six hundred miles off the Japanese coast by fishing boats serving as patrol craft. The light cruiser *Nashville*, with fifteen six-inch guns in five turrets, three forward and two aft, looked the picture of naval warfare in the age of steam as she came up to flank speed—about thirty-five knots—turned sharply to port, and began firing. Signal flags crackled as they ran up and down on the halyards, black smoke blew in the wind, yellow flashes came out of the gun barrels, and salvo after salvo missed the little boats bobbing on the waves, now in sight, now hidden. They were not easy targets, and the rounds that hit were armor piercing and went through the wooden hulls without exploding. The *Nashville* sailors stubbornly denied over the years that their gunnery had failed and that the transfer of their ship to the Aleutians soon afterward was a removal to a less critical area, but it looked like a big failure to the sailors on other ships.

It was assumed that the Japanese had radioed alerts to Tokyo, though they hadn't, and although the range was a hundred miles or so too long for the B-25s, the decision was made to risk it and launch anyway. So turning into a wind that was now close to forty knots, which helped the launch, the *Hornet* began to send the bombers off. The first plane, Doolittle's, didn't even use up the available deck. So powerful was the effect of the wind added to the full speed of the ship—about seventy-five knots total—that the B-25s needed only to get up about thirty knots' speed to float off the deck like great kites, only slowly moving ahead of the ship, which seemed to remain almost stationary below them. One after another the entire squadron went off, and we all cheered loudly and choked down a few patriotic tears. I thought my ten dollars well lost in a good cause, as if I had actually contributed the money to success in the war. We turned back at once to get out of range of Japanese aircraft, and although we were told that Doolittle had bombed Tokyo, we heard no details about how most of the planes made it to China until years afterward, when the entire story of the minor damage, but heavy blow to Japanese pride, became public.

Within a few days it was warm again, and after another brief stop at Pearl we departed, still with the *Hornet,* for the southwest Pacific, where the battle to contain a Japanese drive to the south and the east—Australia, New Guinea, and the Solomon Islands—was shaping up. Task forces centered on aircraft carriers maneuvered to locate the enemy and get in the first strike before being discovered. Two of our fleet carriers in the Pacific, the *Lexington* and *Yorktown,* were already in the Coral Sea, off the eastern end of New Guinea, trying to block two Japanese fleets coming at them from opposing directions. We were being sent to equal the odds and coming in from the east to surprise a Japanese two-carrier task force coming south from Truk.

Wartime cruising now became a routine in which boredom and tiredness ate away at the usual good nature of sailors. Stripped of paint and linoleum, rusting everywhere, hot from cruising near the equator, with only a few air blowers open below deck, shuddering from high-speed maneuvers in a way that knocked over anything set on shelves and tables, the ships and the life aboard them began to get to us. Fresh food lasted only a few days after we had been in port; we washed and shaved in salt water, our skin irritated by sandy saltwater soap; work and catnaps filled up the days. Dungarees and blue work shirts, the standard uniform of the day, were never ironed, only washed and dried all together in a great bag that had to be rummaged through to find the pieces with your name stenciled on them. Put on clean and dry, they were soaking wet from sweat in a few minutes. White hats were dyed an anemic purple, and white socks were forbidden so as to avoid flashes of white on the flight deck that would betray the presence of the ship to snooper aircraft. Heat rash tormented everyone, particularly around the waist, where several layers of wet clothing twisted and scraped inside a belt. A story circulated that you would die when the heat rash—a quarter of an inch high and several inches wide, red and angry—had girdled your waist. No one believed it, but everyone kept a careful eye on the progress of the rash around his middle. Every free moment was spent somewhere the cooling breeze could blow over the rash and the sun could dry it out. Lacking any movies, radio, or music to entertain us, we gambled. It became the only relief from the tedium of what was now becoming not weeks but months at sea without even a sight of land in the distance. I was a more enthusiastic than skillful poker player, but I loved the game, as I did bridge, and even though I regularly lost my money in small games in out-of-the-way compartments around the ship, the first glimpse of the five cards in draw poker or the hole card in stud poker were the highest moments, ironically, of days that were routinely filled with accidents and sometimes death.

Death lived on an aircraft carrier operating in wartime conditions. One day a plane would crash taking off, and a lucky pilot lost no more than an eye on the telescopic sight mounted in front of him. The next day a plane landing on deck would drop a wheel strut into the catwalk and run screeching up it for a hundred feet. A mangled crewman who had been watching the landing would be carried away. A thoughtless step backward on the flight and hangar decks where the planes were turning up led to decapitation and gory dismemberment by a propeller. Planes went out on patrol and were never heard of again. Death took many forms, but I think I first really came to know him on a day when I was standing on the flight deck and a Dauntless dive-bomber flew across the ship to drop a message. Once ships had put to sea, strict radio silence was maintained except for certain high-frequency TBS (short-range Talk Between Ships). Beanbags trailing long red streamers were used by planes for message drops in order to preserve radio silence. As the dive-bomber came across the ship at about 120 knots, with the starboard wing sharply down to give the radioman an open field to throw the message bag on the flight deck, the down wing caught, ever so slightly, just a tick, the railing of the catwalk at the very edge of the ship. It was enough. In an instant the plane was in the water off the starboard side, broken in half between the radioman and the pilot, neither of whom, knocked out by the crash, heads hanging limply forward, moved. Then in an instant both pieces were gone, the water was unruffled, and the ship sailed on. How quickly life swooping along in the graceful plane disappeared as if it had never been! It was the instantaneous succession of quite a lot of something and nothing that focused my attention, and like some eighteen-year-old ancient mariner, I went around for days trying to tell people what had really happened, how astounding it was. The response was polite; death was a grave matter and never lightly dismissed. But no one, quite rightly, wanted to philosophize or make too much of what was common and likely to be the end of all of us, much sooner than later.

FIVE

Midway

The embers of fear of death that never left us were fanned to life a few days later when we heard that the *Lexington,* commissioned in the early 1920s, had been sunk and the *Yorktown* damaged by aircraft in the Battle of the Coral Sea, the first of the great carrier battles of the Pacific war. The *Lexington* was a "good ship," as was said in the navy—while her sister ship, the *Saratoga,* was not, for unknown reasons—and the news of her sinking was felt as a personal blow, particularly by the many aboard the *Enterprise* (a relatively new ship, commissioned in 1938) who had served on the "Lady Lex." Felt too because she was the first American fleet carrier to go down—CV-1, the old *Langley,* had been sunk in Indonesia, but she was only a converted coal carrier—making clear our own vulnerability by increasing the ratio to six Japanese carriers against only three American.

Our desire for revenge was thwarted when the *Enterprise* and *Hornet* turned and began making a high-speed run back to Pearl Harbor. It seemed to us like craven cowardice, once again, and there was a good deal of muttering. But as we approached Pearl, where there was, we were told, to be no liberty this time, scuttlebutt began to whisper a fantastic story. We had broken the Japanese code, it was said, and learned that their fleet was about to attack Midway Island, with a diversionary move on the Aleutians. We were going to lie off Midway and ambush them. I remember the exact occasion on which I was told, with plentiful details about ships and dates, about the coming battle, but intelligence officers still insist that secrecy on this critical matter was carefully maintained. Everyone who has been in the service, particularly the navy, can testify that it is impossible to keep a secret, no matter how big—messages have to pass through too many hands and be seen by too many eyes—and I repeat that among the enlisted men it was widely known before Midway that we had broken the Japanese code, and the strategy and tactics for the coming battle were learnedly discussed by the admirals of the lower deck, who were, on the whole, of the opinion, as always, that the officers would screw it up.

A few days out of Pearl a destroyer came alongside with the mail that was our lifeline to familiarity. Several hours later the letters worked their way down to the divisional compartments and were passed out by the mail orderly who stood cracking jokes in the center of an anxious circle of impatient sailors: "Smith, she's run off with a marine." My best letters came from my mother, who was a good correspondent, typing long and interesting letters about the dogs, cats, and horses on the ranch, telling me about the neighbors and the plans for the spring and new buildings. I saved her letter for later and opened first a letter from my stepfather (he did not often write), dated April 28, 1942. The words hit me like a hammer: "I am writing this in Saratoga on Sunday morning following the funeral of our Dear. . . . I went over to get in the wood and do the chores. The door was locked. My first thought was it was a joke. I called to her and no answer. Then I tapped the door with my overshoe and asked to be let in. No answer. Then I got alarmed and kicked the door in. Mother was laying in the dining room Dead. I ran to her and felt her pulse. She was cold as marble. I felt her head and it was likewise. She had shot herself in the temple with the 22 pistol you gave her. I did not touch the gun. The whole sight was one awful shock and I will not describe the scene further in this letter. I hunted for a note for a few minutes and then lit out for town. I ran until I was ready to keel and then got control of myself to go into a walk."

The old letter still has burns from when I crumpled it and put it in a bulkhead ashtray before I finished reading, only to return to dig it out, smoldering, and go through each of the awful details. I opened the letter from my mother later, hoping for some clue to what had happened. It was written a few days before her suicide on April 22 and gave no indication that anything in particular was wrong. Apparently she had bottled up whatever it was, as she always had. In all the old photos she was always hard to spot in the group, lurking in the background, away in the corner. Her suicide was, of course, ultimately rooted in despair, despair over all the many things that had gone wrong in her life and could never be put right, despair from living on an isolated ranch with no company; but I hunted for particular reasons, blaming myself for having left her and sending Jane the other postcard.

The telegram telling me of Mother's death arrived in the mail months later. On a ship in the middle of an ocean, on the way to a great battle, trying to deal with a faraway death, the body already buried a month earlier, creates overwhelming emotional pressure. Having to do something, I blundered down into the pale-green officers' quarters, where enlisted men were prohibited without a pass, and found my way to the Catholic chaplain's rooms. I was not devout, but I had been raised a Catholic, and now seemed the time, if ever, to call on religion for help not to be found elsewhere. The chaplain was napping. Startled to see a tearful young sailor, he asked first if I had a pass to be in officers' country, which I did not. Being young, I expected help, and insisted that he provide it in some tangible form like getting me leave to go home, which he could not, of course, arrange.

The chief of the ordnance gang, Murphy, sipping his customary moosemilk, was more sympathetic and more practical. He took me off mess cooking—sending some other poor devil down to the galleys—and gave me a day off, which I spent sitting on a sponson and staring at the ocean rolling by and trying to think of some answer to my sorrow. I slept unexpectedly well that night, which made me feel guilty but began in the way of living things to heal my grief.

A second day off was not thought good for me by the assembled wisdom of the ordnance gang, sitting in solemn conclave like a consistory of cardinals, wearing the red-cloth helmets, that were the symbol of our trade. So somber but glad to have escaped from mess cooking, I was put to work again along with everyone else, getting ammunition up from the magazines, taking it out of its wooden boxes, opening the greased tin inner containers and paper cartons, and then using hand- and automatic belting machines to shove the bullets into the connecting metal links to feed the machine guns of the planes in the coming battle. Black tips were armor piercing; blue, incendiary; red, tracer; and plain, ball. We made up different combinations for different purposes, using more tracer where it was important to be able to see from the burning base of the bullet where the fire stream was going, more armor piercing and incendiary for the hits, and ball to keep the barrels of the guns from burning out too quickly with all this hard, hot stuff.

While I was working away, eating, sleeping, and in a short time talking and joking with the rest of the ordnance gang, my mother's death drifted away from consciousness. I found, like many another, that we are much simpler mechanisms than we think, preserving life and accepting whatever shreds of meaning we can find in it. The dead must bury the dead because the living do not—cannot—pause long enough to do so. Guilt for the dead, especially a suicide, is powerful, but the danger, I soon found, is in feeling that you cannot move away from it and thus letting deep emotions become too tangled.

On May 26 we were back in Pearl. Halsey, who had been standing for weeks on the bridge in his skivvies trying to cool the allergic rash that was covering his body—he must have been more nervous than he appeared to be—went to the hospital on shore. He had become a hero to the crew by then, for no apparent good reason except that he was gruff and outspoken, and his departure seemed ominous. Nimitz came aboard, and we all stood to quarters to watch medals presented to various worthies. Later, Spruance, not an aviator, came aboard as the new admiral commanding Task Force 16, built around the *Enterprise* and *Hornet,* for the Battle of Midway.

Though no one else got liberty, someone saw fit to give me a two-hour compassionate liberty after we reached Pearl, enough time to race into Honolulu in a taxi to the Mackay office (naval communications were never used for personal matters—maybe for officers, I wouldn't know, but never for enlisted men) to cable some borrowed money home to help with funeral expenses and let my stepfather know that his letter had been received, that grief had spread as far as it was likely to for this death. The brass would never have let me off the ship, let alone into a cable office, if they thought I or anyone else had the slightest knowledge about the Japanese plans and the coming battle. How astounded they would have been to learn that everyone in the crew knew about the code and the plans! All precautions were taken to seal off the ship lest something leak out somehow, and I was always grateful to whoever made the eloquent argument that must have been necessary to get me ashore under those tense circumstances.

The time in port was short, two days, and filled with all-hands details: provisioning the ship, filling the magazines, getting stores and fuel aboard. Despite the blackout, bright floodlights burned all night as one lighter after another came alongside, while workmen installed new guns and equipment. But no one complained, for once, about extra duty, and excitement shone in everyone's eyes. By the late morning of the 28th of May, barges alongside still casting off, we, along with the *Hornet,* were under way, steaming once again out of that deep channel that leads south out of the big harbor at Pearl to open water. The *Yorktown* was still being patched up in the dry dock at Pearl and would follow in a few days to complete the American fleet. Though we were unaware of it, at the same time (May 29, Japanese time), the commander of the Japanese Imperial Fleet, Isoruku Yamamoto, on his flagship *Yamato,* the largest ship in the world—seventy thousand tons, nine 18.1-inch guns—was taking the Japanese fleet out of Yashiro-jima through the Bungo Channel on the way to Midway, twenty-five-hundred miles to the east.

Once under way, we continued belting machine-gun ammunition obsessively, like some rite of war, piling up huge mounds ready for use in the planes. We also piled up an enormous amount of trash that had to be burned: long tow targets filled with pasteboard cartridge cartons pulled like Chinese festival dragons laboriously down the passageways and ladders to the ship's incinerator to be burned at night, when the smoke would not give away the position of the ship to submarines or scout planes. Someone had to shovel this mountain of trash into the incinerator far below decks, and perhaps because of recent favors shown me I was dispatched to shovel tons of paper into the incinerator all night long. The job required two sailors, dressed only in skivvies in the boiling heat that was filled with the stale smell of trash, flames weirdly lighting the small space. The cardboard contained bullets here and there that had been missed in the sorting, and after these had lain in the hot fire for a time they exploded. Since they had no backing when they went off, the bullets lacked the force to go through the insulated steel sides of the furnace, but if by chance one came through the door of the incinerator when it was open, it would maim anyone it hit. One man opened the door of the furnace and ducked while the other sailor threw a shovel load in the furnace and then quickly dropped to the deck to avoid any rounds that might have cooked off since the last shovelful was thrown in. The pops were loud and frequent, and shovel-drop-pop from sunset to sunrise jangled the nerves.

We were under heavier fire than the rest of the crew, but the frustration of being occupied with trash disposal while going into what we all knew would be one of the big naval battles of all time kept us from feeling heroic.

After burning trash all night, I went up to the ordnance shack on the morning of June 4 to help put the torpedoes on the planes. Incinerator or not, I wasn't going to miss out on this one. This was the big day when U.S. naval air tactics that had been developed over twenty years were at last going to be put into practice. Knowing that the Japanese fleet intended to attack and take Midway to prevent Doolittle-type raids and draw out our fleet for the big surface battle they believed would end the war, the three American carriers—the *Enterprise,* the *Hornet,* and the battered *Yorktown,* all sister ships and the only American carriers left in the central Pacific—had steamed more than a thousand miles and joined to the north and east of Midway at the aptly named Point Luck. Though we were apprehensive, the Japanese were completely unaware of our presence. Having beaten us so easily for so long, they were careless with their scouting and launched half of their planes for a land attack on Midway. Their position was established just after dawn by PBY Catalinas flying out of Midway. Our carriers turned into the wind, and the *Enterprise* and *Hornet* began to launch their strike at about 0700. The *Yorktown* held back its strike for an hour until it was sure that there were not other Japanese carriers shadowing the main force.

All the ground crew, aware that this was the big day, were out to see the pilots and crews off, and as he walked by Winchell, one of the squadron's several enlisted pilots who had recently been made warrant officers, made me proud by borrowing my cigarette lighter for luck. The commander of the squadron, Lt. Cdr. E. E. Lindsey, was taped from his waist to his neck following a crash a few days earlier: bad eyesight had caused him to try to land at an odd angle to the flight deck. But he would not give up the battle. When it was suggested that he should stay in sick bay on the day of the attack, he replied, "This is what I have been trained to do," and led his squadron into the greatest sea battle of the century, in which he and most of his men died.

The dive-bombers of Bombing 6 and Scouting 6, thirty-three in all, went off first, the scouts with two one-hundred-pound bright yellow bombs under the wings and a five-hundred-pounder under the fuselage, the bombers with a single yellow one-thousand-pounder. After a long interval during which no other planes got off because of a mix-up on the deck, the bombers were ordered to proceed independently toward target on a course of 231 degrees, distance 142 miles. This plot assumed that Nagumo, the vice-admiral of the Japanese navy, would maintain his course toward Midway, but he turned north to 70 degrees when he recovered his Midway strike, and therefore our bombers flew too far south. The torpedo planes, fourteen TBDs, were on their way next. Each carried two men, the pilot and the radioman-gunner. The mid-seat observer-bombardiers were left behind that day, to save weight and lives, for everyone knew that whatever happened, it was going to be a bad day for the misnamed "Devastators."

We all knew that a new, much improved torpedo plane, the Grumman TBF, was ready for the fleet. One section of the *Hornet* torpedo squadron (VT-8) had already gotten the new planes, and six of them had flown out to Midway, and from there they too attacked the Japanese fleet on June 4, though with no better success than the carrier squadrons. After the torpedo planes, ten fighters went into the air to provide protection from the Japanese fighter planes, the remarkable Zeros, which would be among the lumbering torpedo planes before they came within range of the antiaircraft guns of the Japanese fleet.

Timing and communication were everything in a carrier aircraft strike, but despite years of practice, both broke down from the start. The *Enterprise* squadrons were separated at the outset when the dive bombers went off alone on the wrong course, delaying their arrival at the target until after the torpedo planes had made their run. The torpedo planes took off by themselves to find the Japanese fleet. Low on gas by the time they got to the Japanese carriers after 0900, they started their attack at once, without any dive-bombers or fighters in sight. The fighters, high above, mistakenly identified Torpedo 8 from the *Hornet* as their charge, but didn't help them either. They remained at high altitude where there were no Japanese fighters, as they had all gone down to shoot up the TBDs from sea level; and while VT-6 was dying, the fighters decided that there was no opposition that day and turned around and flew back to the *Enterprise*. Unhindered, the Zeros closed in on the torpedo planes as they began their runs and shot down nine of the fourteen. None of our torpedoes hit, or if they did they did not explode.

The *Enterprise* strike was supposed to take place at the same time that planes from the *Hornet* attacked other Japanese carriers. But things were far worse on the *Hornet* than they were on the *Enterprise*. Cdr. Stanhope Ring, the leader of the *Hornet* air group, led his planes far north of the Japanese fleet, a massive error in navigation that has still not been explained. His bombers returned with their bombs still in their racks, his fighters broke off and ditched when they ran out of gas, his Torpedo 8 squadron, led by Lt. Cdr. John Waldron, broke off early from the group, left the "flight to nowhere," flew directly to the Japanese carriers, attacked, and died, everyone except the famous Ensign Gay.

Only the *Yorktown,* wiser from experience at the Battle of the Coral Sea, sent its planes directly to the Japanese. But the *Yorktown* torpedo squadron, Torpedo 3, had no better luck than the other Devastators, despite being accompanied by both fighters and dive-bombers that attacked simultaneously. Ten of twelve torpedo planes were shot down, again without an explosion on a carrier hull; two made it back to their ship but had to land in the water.

The *Enterprise* dive-bombers eventually found the Japanese carriers and joined with the *Yorktown* Dauntlesses—arriving at the same time by good luck, not planning—to sink three of them, coming at them in classic style, out of the sun. It was over in fifteen minutes, at around 1030. The three Japanese carriers went up like tinder. And in the afternoon the bombers went back and finished off the fourth and last carrier. Four of the six carriers that had carried out the attack on Pearl Harbor—*Kaga, Akagi, Hiryu,* and *Soryu*—were all burning by evening and would sink before the next morning.

In this famous victory the torpedo planes played an unintended and unforeseen part. The deck-spotting procedures of the Japanese carriers, referred to earlier, required about forty-five minutes to get their bombers and torpedo planes up from the hangar decks and send them out to attack the American fleet. But the torpedo plane attacks forced them to keep their flight decks clear to launch and land fighters, maintaining the maximum number of armed Zeros in the air to deal with the feared torpedo planes. As a result the Japanese could not find time to prepare strikes against the American fleet. Had they been able to do so our losses would surely have been great, for the one strike the Japanese did send out from the carrier that escaped sinking in the first round managed to cripple the *Yorktown.* No one can claim credit for this critical achievement, totally unintended and unheralded for sixty years, except the aircrews whose blazing courage and sense of duty drove them to fly their old planes with their defective torpedoes to a desperate end without flinching.

In the late morning we waited for our planes on the deck of the *Enterprise,* with an eye toward the *Hornet* nearby and the *Yorktown* several miles away to the west. Our fighters came back first, intact, which seemed odd, and then one, two, three, and finally four torpedo planes straggled in separately, and that was it. The last of the planes was so badly shot up that it was deep-sixed immediately after it landed. One pilot, Winchell, and his radioman, Douglas Cossitt, were later picked up out of the water, sixty pounds lighter following seventeen days adrift in a raft. The total losses for our squadron alone were nine out of fourteen crews.

The loss was unimaginable, and even when the survivors, in a condition of shock, told us what kind of a slaughter it had been, it was hard to believe. It came closer to home when one of the surviving torpedo pilots, a bushy-mustached warrant officer named Smith, came out of his cockpit brandishing his .45 automatic and charged up the ladder to the bridge shouting that he was going to kill the lieutenant, James Gray, who had commanded the fighter escort. He was prevented by force from doing it, but the whole scandal was out in an instant that the torpedo planes had attacked alone. The matter has remained an issue in naval aviation to this day, and in 1988 Capt. James Gray rose at a conference on Midway to change his story and declare that he and his fighters had not been able to protect the torpedo planes because the new types of fighters they flew, the F4F-4s, were heavier than the older F4F-3s and guzzled an unexpected amount of gas. But on the *Enterprise* on the morning of June 4, 1942, there was no doubt that the fighters had failed badly, and the torpedo planes had paid the price.

Around noon came the clanging alarm, the bugle call, "All hands man your battle stations," and then a few minutes later, "Bandits at twenty miles and closing, stand by to repel enemy air attack." But we were not the target that day. The *Yorktown*, about ten miles to port, was between us and the Japanese fleet, and it took the full weight of the attack. How glad we secretly were that it was not us. We stood on the deck and watched, as if it were a movie, the flashes and smoke from the antiaircraft guns in the distance. The *Yorktown* heeled over in sharp turns, taking evasive action, while near misses exploded around her. Attacking and defending planes blew up in bright flares. Not all the bombs missed, and when it was over in less than half an hour, the *Yorktown* was down on the port side, dead in the water, and there were holes in her flight deck large enough to make it impossible for her to land her own planes. She was patched up and by 1400 was moving under her own power again, only to be hit by two torpedoes launched in the second and last Japanese strike from the fourth carrier, *Hiryu,* missed in the morning but dispatched soon afterward. Even then she didn't go down until a submarine finished her off on the morning of June 7.

Within a few minutes after the first attack on the *Yorktown,* her dive-bombers and ours began arriving in small clusters and singly. Shot up, some landing in the water, out of gas, some crashing on deck with failing landing gear or no tailhooks and immediately being pushed over the side to make room for the others coming in. But now the mood was triumphant. The bomber pilots could hardly contain themselves. They were shouting and laughing as they jumped out of the cockpits, and the ship that had been so somber a moment before when the torpedo planes returned now became hysterically excited. We were exultant, not just at the revenge for Pearl Harbor, sweet as that was, but at our renewed sense of power and superiority over the Japanese fleet. No one doubted by now that it would be a long war, but to everyone on the ships at Midway it was clear that we would win.

But a lot of faith in our equipment was swept away on June 4. For one, our torpedo planes, the old TBDs, were undeniably death traps, slow, under-armed, and lacking in maneuverability. The Zeros had shot them down at will, not only the *Enterprise* squadron but also the squadrons from the *Yorktown* and *Hornet.* Even the detached group with the new planes, the TBFs and the army B-26s, lost five of the six TBFs and two of the four B-26s flying from Midway. Put it all together and 51 planes had tried to hit the Japanese ships with torpedoes that day. Only 7 landed back at base. This comes to an aircraft loss rate of 86 percent. Out of 124 pilots and crew who were in torpedo planes, 28—including 12 from the army planes—survived; 96 died. VT-8, the *Hornet* squadron, became famous for losing all of its 15 planes and all its men except Ensign Gay, who flew over the carrier he was attacking and crashed on the other side but managed to get out and hide under a cushion in his life jacket. His ashes were spread years later near the point where the torpedo squadrons died so valiantly.

If any of the planes got a hit, they had no effect, for the torpedoes were erratic and either broke up, porpoised, exploded early, or failed to explode. The failure of our torpedoes in planes and submarines during the first three years of the war—which everyone in the fleet knew and talked about—and the refusal of the administrators to acknowledge the problem and fix it, remains one of the scandals of the U.S. Navy. All that reckless heroism with no chance of success even if things had gone well, instead of going about as badly as they could.

Our fighters showed up little better. The Grumman F4F-4s were no match for the Zeros at Midway. Lieutenant Laub, the senior surviving officer of Torpedo 6, remarked sadly that even if our fighters had supported the squadron it would have made no difference because they were inferior to the Zeros. He was right, for the six fighters from the *Yorktown* that accompanied its torpedo planes, led by the famous Jimmy Thach, were driven off by the Japanese fighters after losing one plane.

It was the dive-bombers that emerged at Midway as the primary weapon of naval aviation, and until the end of the war, dive- or glide-bombing with one type of plane or another remained our most effective tactic. Thirty-three dive-bombers in the *Enterprise* group and half that number in the *Yorktown* group were enough to do what was needed. Even their success, however, turned not on planning so much as on luck and a piece of rare good judgment by Lt. Cdr. Wade McClusky, the commander of Air Group 6. Having gone to the point of no return without sighting the Japanese—who had turned north when they discovered the American fleet on their flank—he decided to go on for another ten minutes, during which time he saw the wake of a Japanese destroyer eighteen thousand feet below going northeast. He chose to follow it, and over the horizon saw *Kido Butai,* the mighty Japanese attack fleet, below him, its

Combat Air Patrol all down at sea level shooting up the torpedo planes. When Bombing 5 from the *Yorktown* arrived a little later, the bombers went to work together. I have always thought that if there were one single crucial act in the Pacific war it was Wade McClusky's turn northeast, and although I never saw him after he landed, I have often wished him a long and prosperous life.

Battles are well planned, but their outcomes regularly turn on chance. So it was at Midway, for the Japanese as well as the Americans. A fatal overconfidence engendered by victories in the early months of the war no doubt contributed to negligence on their part, but accident also played a crucial role. One of their scouts from a cruiser was late being launched on the morning of June 4 and just happened to be the scout assigned to the sector in which our fleet was located. So, still unaware of our presence, the Japanese prepared for a second strike against Midway, thinking that they had all the time in the world. When they finally learned that we were there they began frantically rearming for a strike against our carriers. But first they brought the earlier strike, low on gas, back aboard, intending to send a full-load strike from all four carriers against us. But it was too late. The Japanese were brave men, but it is hard not to exult across fifty years upon reading about the shouts of their lookouts ("Hell Divers!") and their panic as the crews looked up into the sun and saw the dive-bombers there, with the bombs already in the air beneath the planes on their way into the big red rising suns painted on their yellow flight decks. Hard too not to admire the fatalism with which their great pilot and air planner, Cdr. Minoru Genda, met the disaster, with the brief word *Shimatta,* "We goofed."

At the end of the first day of battle the *Enterprise* pilots and those from the *Yorktown* who had landed on the *Enterprise* after sinking the Japanese carriers stood in a long line, waiting to be debriefed, just outside the incinerator where I was back to lighting up for the night's inferno and preparing to duck the slow bullets that hadn't made it to the battle. These were heroes, dressed in their khaki and green nylon flight suits, carrying pistols and knives over their yellow Mae Wests, and describing with quick hands and excited voices how they had gone into their dives, released their bombs, and seen the Japanese flight decks open up in flames just below them. The slaves who rowed the Greek warriors at Salamis or those chained to their benches at Lepanto could not have felt at once prouder or less heroic than I.

The Battle of Midway was fought and won in ninety minutes on the morning of June 4, and it was finished by sunset, when the last of the four Japanese carriers, the *Hiryu,* was gutted. Before withdrawing, the Japanese tried to force a night surface action, but we retreated, and the next day we came back to grapple for their remaining ships. An information officer on the *Enterprise* tried to chalk a map on the huge gray side of the stack so that all on deck could follow the battle—we were fascinated at the new idea of being briefed—but every fifteen minutes the man on the painting scaffold suspended from the top of the stack chalked up a new location and a different size for the fleets. As the information constantly changed and the proximity to the enemy increased or decreased, so did the armaments. Bomb size went from one-thousand-pounders to five-hundreds and back again on the dive-bombers within the space of an hour. This meant endless work for ordnancemen, which at last got me out of the incinerator. I had just been made a petty officer, third class (sixty dollars a month), a certified professional, and I happily ran back and forth trundling bombs and carrying belted ammunition for the machine guns, a part of the ordnance gang again. Aware that this was probably the greatest historical event at which I would ever be present, I looked about for something to fix Midway in my mind forever. I was waiting on the flight deck for a bomb to come up the forward bomb elevator shaft, which was about three feet by four. I looked down the narrow shaft going several hundred feet from the bright sunlight of the day into the depths of the ship, where, close to the keel, the bomb magazines were located. At the very bottom, a bright yellow bomb had just been wheeled on the elevator, so that I was looking down an immensely long tunnel at a bright yellow spot, at once both beautiful and deadly, at the bottom. To this moment I can see it as clearly as if I were still there.

Nothing in the next two days of the battle could match the first, although the excitement remained high and the level of activity feverish. The Japanese fleet proved elusive. We caught only a couple of cruisers and destroyers and hammered them viciously. Our remaining three Devastators were loaded for the last time with torpedoes and sent out on the hunt, but they were not needed and circled the fight without making a run. Without their carriers the Japanese fleet returned home, where news of the battle was suppressed and the crews were kept aboard their ships lest they talk of what had happened. The *Enterprise* returned to Pearl Harbor on the morning of June 13, my nineteenth birthday.

SIX

Sunk

After Midway we were a squadron without pilots or planes. When we returned to Pearl Harbor, the enlisted men of Torpedo 6 were sent to the naval air station at Kaneohe, on the windward side of Oahu, where a new set of pilots with a new type of plane were waiting for us. The few surviving pilots from the old squadron had gone back to the States and, except for a few old hands, the new ones were fresh from flight training and eager to get into the war. Among the old hands was the famous Lt. (jg) John McInerny. He had been a fighter pilot on the *Hornet* at Midway, and on the "flight to nowhere" he had the brass to fly up to his squadron commander, who was calmly proceeding into oblivion, and point to the gas gauge to remind him they had reached the point of no return. Preserving radio silence, the skipper vigorously motioned McInerny back to his place in the formation. But after a few seconds, Mac was back, even more insistent, and the skipper this time ignored him, doubtless thinking something like, "Get your insubordinate Irish ass back where it belongs." But McInerny was a determined realist, and he and his wingman, Johnny Magda, broke away from the fighter formation to return to the ship. After a few moments the rest of the group did the same, and finally the skipper turned back too. They all missed the ship and flew on above an empty ocean until they ran out of gas and ditched. Eight of the ten, Mac among them, were later picked up after several days floating in the ocean. But he was through in fighters and had been sent to fly torpedo planes, a considerable comedown in the aviators' world. He died of cancer in 1986, a great loss to courage and good sense.

The new plane was the Grumman TBF, called the "Avenger," to avenge what had happened to the torpedo planes at Midway. It looked like the latest thing in aviation technology to us. Heavy bodied, with square folding wings, light-blue and white outside, dark green inside, it carried three men, but the radio gunner was now down in a little compartment at the rear of the plane. Above him and slightly forward was the gunner's power turret, containing a single .50-caliber machine gun. Stenciled in bright yellow letters on the armor plate that the gunner pulled up when he was in place were the words "Hard Homo." The meaning was quite a mystery, and a lot of time was wasted trying to figure it out. The most obvious meaning, "hard homogenized steel," was disqualified on the grounds that it was so obvious that there would be no reason to stencil it on the thousands of plates put in the turret to protect the gunner's bottom. Every gunner in the fleet must have spent some time in flight wondering just what the words meant.

The pilot eventually had two fifties in the wings. There was another seat forward of the turret just behind the pilot, designed for an observer. It was, in fact, immediately filled up with new radio gear for which there was no room elsewhere. The engine was much more powerful than the one in the old TBDs, and the plane could turn up 180 knots while carrying a torpedo or full bomb load, stored in a long bomb bay in the belly with folding hydraulic doors. Every one of these features was to become grimly familiar to me at one time or another, but for the moment they seemed only wonders of American engineering and production, ingenious ways of beating the Japanese.

The ground crews studied the manuals that came with the new plane, working long days getting used to its ways. We rode in them frequently to see how all the gear worked, from the smoke-laying equipment, which the navy still considered one of its tactical weapons, to the reel that paid out the cable with the tow target that was used for aircraft and ship's gunnery practice. Both of these pieces of equipment were standard, and both were hated by those of us who installed and worked them. The smoke was toxic and acidic enough to burn a pair of dungarees right off your ass, taking the ass with them if you weren't careful. The tow reel, its gears driven by a fiendish little propeller mounted outside on the fuselage, let kinks develop in the tow wire that could, if you were careless, take a hand off when you tried to free them.

Still, it was a wonderful time. Kaneohe, just across the island and over the high cliffs—Nuuanu Pali—from Honolulu, was all soft breezes, big surf, white beaches, and bright sun every day. The barracks were concrete, spacious, clean, and cool. Discipline was incredibly lax, and gambling went on all night in the heads, where the lights burned without interruption. For once I made a few dollars and managed to get an overnight liberty in Honolulu. I soon learned why I had no trouble getting a pass. A curfew cleared the streets at 2000; the restaurants had no food and the bars no whiskey. I had a good time, however, renting a room in the posh though empty Alexander Young Hotel downtown, lying in a marble bath smoking a cigar and reading the *Police Gazette,* as naughty a magazine as I could find, but not very naughty.

Promotion was also easy too in an expanding navy. Ratings were now given away with a stroke of a yeoman's typewriter, to the disgust of the old-timers who had laboriously studied manuals and waited years for promotion. There was an argument in the ordnance shack one day about who would go down to the beach and fill some of the practice bombs with sand. No one wanted to go, heavy jobs with shovels being scrupulously avoided in the navy—if you liked that sort of thing there was always the army—and so Murph said that he would make me a petty officer, second class, if I would do it without bellyaching. I thought he was joking, but I did it anyway, and the next week the squadron orders listed my name and the new rating of aviation ordnanceman, second class, paying the munificent sum of seventy-four dollars a month.

At Kaneohe I drifted into a part-time flying arrangement. All regular flight personnel drew additional half-pay, known as "flight skins." The squadron had a few extra sets of skins beyond those needed for the regular pilots and flight crews, and these were passed around among the leading chiefs and various personnel from time to time. Even little fish like me had a chance to get a half or a quarter skin once in a rare while. But you had to put in at least four certified hours a month in the air to qualify. The flight logs were sacred books not to be tampered with, and so actual flight time could not be avoided. Sometimes planes were crammed with ten or twelve persons flying around the island for four hours to get their flight time in.

The new planes had a turret with a .50-caliber machine gun, but there were as yet no specially qualified aerial gunners. It was assumed, however, that any ordnanceman could at least operate the turret and the gun, even if he couldn't hit a barn door. So from time to time, needing to put in a few hours in the air, I became a gunner, complete with a helmet, earphones, a khaki flight suit, and a leather flight jacket with my name and rating stamped in gold on a patch on the breast. Other ordnancemen remembered the lesson of Midway, and I had little competition for a job of which I was exceedingly proud. Most of the time, though, I worked away on the ground: cleaned guns, bore sighted the fixed guns, loaded bombs and torpedoes, unloaded bombs and torpedoes.

The idyll was over in a month or so, and in late July we packed up and went back to Pearl to go aboard, not the *Enterprise,* which had already sailed for the South Pacific, but the *Hornet.* The old system of keeping air groups and ships together—Air Group 6 went with CV-6, the *Enterprise;* Air Group 5 went with CV-5, the *Yorktown*—around which fierce loyalties were built, was no longer possible: the carriers now took whatever squadrons were trained and available when they sailed. Airedales like us became vagabonds from this time on. Squadrons were seldom again at home on a particular ship, or even in an air group.

Torpedo Squadron 6 was for the moment a part of the *Hornet* Air Group, which was made up of squadrons with various numbers. Because of our loyalty to the *Enterprise* we did not take to the *Hornet*. She was new and had come into the Pacific for the Doolittle Raid, and the paint had never been chipped off her bulkheads, so we now had to turn to on a second ship and spend weeks in the sweaty heat with chipping hammer and wire brush. The *Hornet's* crew did not take to us either, but it soon ceased to matter, and since the *Enterprise* and *Hornet* were sister ships we could even have the same bunks in the same compartments we had had on the *Enterprise*. Still, it was different and therefore unsettling.

There still remained, it turned out, one part-time general detail I had not been on—everybody went the full round—and now each time a plane landed or took off, I stood at the edge of the flight deck, just aft of the island, dressed in a huge cumbersome floppy white asbestos suit, complete with boots and a heavy helmet with a glass visor to see through. You carried the helmet since it had no air supply, and you would suffocate in it in a few minutes. In my other hand I had a long chain with a hook at the end. If a plane with a bomb or depth charge aboard crashed and either caught fire or was in danger of catching fire, I put on the helmet, rushed under the plane, and secured the chain around the bomb. At the same time another man, also dressed in an asbestos suit, climbed up the wing of the plane to the cockpit and released the bomb. It then, in theory, fell to the deck, did not explode, and was pulled by my chain, which a number of volunteers had presumably taken hold of, out of the fire and the danger of explosion.

The whole drill had a desperate sound to it, and the asbestos suit had a number of seams and openings that I thought would surely let the fire get to me. My repeated, increasingly insistent questions about this matter got no answers from anyone in charge, and week after week I stood at the aft end of the island, by the mobile crane for clearing wrecks, looking and feeling like a circus clown, hat under arm, getting ready to perform. During the time I was on this detail planes crashed, and I rushed in and hooked the chain on the bomb, but fortunately there was no fire. Never in my time in the service did I see anyone test one of these Daniel suits in a fiery furnace, and I think it just as well.

The ship was hot, but the nights were clear and cool, with a warm light breeze blowing on the flight deck. Everybody off watch congregated on the deck, walking up and down like shadows, stopping here and there to talk. The stars were brilliant, and the sky was crowded with them. The southern heavens were now visible, and the different constellations made it seem as if we had steamed into a world other than that presided over by the North Star and the Big Dipper. After a day at work in the heat, to be on the flight deck at night, cooled by the wind and delighted by the tremendous streams of phosphorescence at the bows of the escort destroyers and cruisers, was more than pleasure. Mostly people on deck at night were silent, but now and then a remarkably free conversation about the meaning of war and life would start with someone you didn't know at all, whose face you couldn't see clearly. Darkness and anonymity were better than daylight for these matters. More open, ironically, and more honest. One day I noticed an unusually earnest member of the squadron, Nelson, lying in his bunk reading *How to Win Friends and Influence People*, the self-improvement book by Dale Carnegie, famous at the time. The foolish title has ensured the book the immortality of true kitsch. I knew it well and saw it again with that sinking feeling that comes from the simultaneous recognition of human need and the futility of trying to satisfy it. My mother, with whom I had had a distant but close relationship, no doubt deeply worried about what was going to happen to a boy with no background and no talent for getting along with people—indeed, almost a genius for the reverse—had made me read it and then quizzed me daily on Dale Carnegie's surefire methods for getting not just along but ahead in the world.

As I walked down the flight deck on some errand a few hours later, Nelson came up alongside me, threw his arm around my shoulder—not done in the navy—and said, "Hey, Al, what's your hometown?" One of Carnegie's basic opening moves. I was thunderstruck. Nelson must surely be an idiot;. here in this topsy-turvy world, where death and mutilation were likely to be in every strange sound and sight, what influence could anyone possibly have that would be of any use? Who were these "friends" to be won? Where? I could only stare at him. The gods of war love nothing more than irony, and to be so blind to where and what we were was downright dangerous. Sure enough, a few days later two of our planes, one carrying Nelson, went into a cloud in close formation and never came out. Even the wreckage was never seen. They must have collided, thrown into each other by heavy up- or downdrafts. I used to wonder whether Nelson thought of winning friends and influencing people as the plane suddenly split open and spilled him out into the air, down to the water below, down to the bottom.

The course was south-southwest, across the equator and down to the southwest Pacific—Australia, the New Hebrides, Rabaul, and the Solomon Islands—where the action had shifted after Midway. This was, by late summer 1942, the farthest reach of the Japanese drive, and it was along the line running from the Solomon Islands to New Guinea that the U.S. Navy had elected to defend the shipping lanes to Australia and stop the Japanese expansion. The marines had gone ashore at Guadalcanal in August, and by the end of that same month the carriers had already fought another of the great carrier-to-carrier battles of the Pacific war, the Battle of the Eastern Solomons. The *Hornet*'s long journey from Pearl Harbor ended at the narrow entrance to the reef outside the harbor of Nouméa, the capital of the French territory of New Caledonia. The island was only semitropical, but it seemed romantic from our anchorage out in the windswept bay, with its long mountain chain running down to the beaches and the forests of palms. Ashore, where we went for a brief liberty, Nouméa was a small French colonial town with a square, a cathedral, a cinema, a few stores, and a rickety racetrack that in time would become only too familiar. There wasn't much to it, but the smells and the architecture were genuinely exotic—white plaster and tile roofs. After a few turns around the square, however, and some ice cream made with coconut milk, the sailors crowded back on the dock to catch the next boat back to the ship. The *Hornet* herself was the biggest attraction in the area. Crowds of sailors who were building a base near Nouméa came out in all kinds of craft to tour the carrier. We were happy to serve as guides—it gave us someone different to talk to—and we felt like real heroes compared to these shore-based sailors. When one friendly group told me as they left to be careful not to get sunk, I was quite surprised; the real possibility had never crossed my mind, and I explained quite earnestly to them that a ship this big and powerful could always take care of herself.

At the beginning of September the *Hornet* joined the *Saratoga* and the *Wasp* patrolling below the Solomons to control the air and keep the two Japanese aircraft carriers that had not been at Midway from coming down from Truk and getting at our ships and the marines on Guadalcanal, a name we began to hear for the first time with the dark tones that have never since left it. The area was so filled with Japanese submarines that it was soon called Torpedo Junction, and a short while later the *Saratoga* was hit by a single torpedo and retired for repairs for the second time in the war. A few days later, up to the north and east of Guadalcanal, we were on routine patrol with the *Wasp*. I had been up all night and had worked through the morning as well, and just after lunch I finally found a cool place in the squadron compartment, several decks down below the hangar deck and well aft. The bunks were kept up during the day, but lying on the deck with a duct blowing cool air across me, I went to sleep, only to be awakened almost at once by general quarters.

Few things were taken so seriously as going at once to your battle station when general quarters was sounded, but we had been having alarms and going to quarters night and day for a week with nothing happening. So I decided "to hell with it" for once, pulled a mattress down to conceal me, and went nicely back to sleep, expecting that the drill would be secured in five or at the most ten minutes and that no one would miss me in the ordnance shack, which was where I was supposed to be. The ship remained deadly quiet, however, and suspecting that something was going on, I made my way by a back route through one watertight hatch after another—court-martial offenses—until I got to the hangar deck. There I looked out through one of the open metal curtains and about a half mile away, down on the port side and to the stern, pouring out huge clouds of black smoke, was the *Wasp*, hit hard and going down from several torpedoes from a Japanese submarine.

Everyone was so focused on the burning ship that I was able to sneak quietly, much subdued, into the ordnance shack. Later the question actually did come up of where I had been because without my knowing it I had been put down to fly that day on the antisubmarine patrol that took off when the *Wasp* was hit. It didn't matter—someone else filled in—and I told a story about being slow and getting trapped behind some watertight doors that couldn't be opened. But it was a dramatic lesson, and I never again failed to respond to general quarters, even when the alarm sounded every hour of the day and night for days at a time, which now became the normal way of life, with frequent reports of submarines and sightings of Japanese scout planes.

Unknown new ships, like the battleship *North Carolina* and the antiaircraft cruisers *Juneau* and *San Juan,* began to show up in the task force, proof that American shipyards were hard at work. But no new carriers. We were now down to one, the *Hornet,* in the South Pacific—the *Enter-*

prise was being repaired—and though the ratio was now three Japanese fleet carriers to one, we raided different Japanese bases and then retired south, once going into Nouméa for supplies. Trying to prevent the Japanese navy from reinforcing and supplying the troops on the Canal and other Solomon islands stretching southeast from New Ireland and the big Japanese base at Rabaul, the U.S. Navy engaged the Japanese in the most ferocious surface battles of the war: cruisers, destroyers, and torpedo boats—even a battleship once in a while—against one another in the dark in the confined waters of "the Slot" between the islands. The Japanese gunnery and tactics were better, especially at night, and we heard of heavy losses, with grim stories of our own cruisers being unprepared for nighttime battles and accidentally firing into one another. "Iron Bottom Bay" became the name of the area between Savo Island and Guadalcanal, where naval gunfire still ruled the ocean—but only at night, when the planes from the "Cactus Air Force" on Henderson Field were grounded.

Tempers grew short and people gave up any attempt to live a normal life. Sandwiches were the standard food, everyone slept where they could with life jackets and helmets nearby, the hatches were dogged down most of the time, the compartments were foul-smelling, and the ship was at general quarters almost constantly. The pilots took to carrying issue sidearms, .45-caliber Colt automatics in a shoulder holster. The heavy guns would weigh them down if they went into the water, but they made them feel more secure should they be shot down and drift ashore on one of the dark little islands that were everywhere on the horizon. I was sent down to the armory one day to draw a case of these antiques from the Spanish-American War—designed to stop Filipino insurrectionists (freedom fighters?) in their tracks—and then sat in the ordnance shack disassembling them, soaking the parts in a solvent to remove the cosmolene in which they had been stored a generation earlier for another enemy, reassembling them, and issuing one gun, plus two clips of ammunition, to any pilot who stopped by to sign for one. If they were sports, they would pay ordnancemen (one of our few cumshaws) to remove the Bakelite handgrips on the butt and put a picture of a girlfriend underneath clear plastic.

The *Enterprise* returned from repairs, running at high speed from Pearl in little more than a week, and on the morning of October 26, 1942, off the Santa Cruz Islands, north and east of the Canal, her search planes found the remaining Japanese fleet carriers, which were coming down from their base at Truk in the Caroline Islands to interfere in the continuing battle between the marines and the Japanese for the possession of the airfield on Guadalcanal. The Japanese fleet was a bit over two hundred miles out, and its scouts found us before we found them.

On the *Hornet,* a few miles from the *Enterprise,* the breeze picked up, as it always did, and the deck vibrated as she turned into the wind and launched the strike group. The planes circled for a time, formed up, and straggled off to the north where a scout plane was broadcasting the location of the enemy fleet, the usual decoy fleet out in front that always seemed to fool our strike groups. The big fleet carriers were about sixty miles behind. A few of our new torpedo planes carried torpedoes but most were now used as glide bombers: "glide" since they couldn't take the steep dive of a dive-bomber but went in at a long medium angle to let their bombs go and then used their speed to get out as fast as possible.

Then both American carriers launched a new CAP, took the morning CAP aboard to be refueled, and immediately sent the planes aloft again to provide a maximum fighter protection against what was surely coming. In the eerie quiet that falls on a carrier after all its planes have gone off on a strike, everyone peered at the horizon. The moments passed as the ship secured from flight quarters and went to general quarters to prepare for the coming attack, sending all bombs and torpedoes to the magazines, emptying the aviation gasoline lines and filling them with CO_2 to prevent fire. Flash burns from explosions had caused many casualties on board ship, and we stuffed our dungarees into our socks, buttoned up our shirt collars and cuffs, put on camphor-impregnated life jackets, smeared any exposed flesh of our hands and faces with a heavy white protective cream, and began to sit and sweat, wearing the old-fashioned World War I helmets, painted navy blue-gray.

Our own strike group and the Japanese sighted each other on their way to their targets, but each passed the other without engaging. I hope they didn't wave, but they may have. By now the hard lesson had been learned by both sides that sinking the enemy carriers was what counted, not shooting down a few planes, so the Americans flew on to find the Japanese ships, the big carriers *Shokaku* and *Zuikaku*—the last two Pearl Harbor carriers—and the Japanese flew on to find the American ships, which they soon did.

A little after 0900, the public address system broke the quiet of the ship with an announcement from the bridge, "Enemy aircraft at fifty miles and closing." In what seemed an unbelievably short time later we heard, "Stand by to repel attack by enemy aircraft," and almost instantly the five-inch guns at the corners of the flight deck began firing—bang-bang-bang—in their heavy slow rhythm, not nearly fast enough it seemed to us. These battles developed speedily, and with the five-inchers still firing, the old navy-built one-point-ones began going off with their much faster but still deliberate rhythm.

In the ordnance shack, just below the flight deck, we could see nothing, only listen, feel the vibrating steel deck, and slide back and forth with the steep turns that came in quick succession. When the new twenty-millimeter guns spaced along the catwalks began their continuous rapid firing, we knew the attack had commenced and that the dive-bombers were coming down and the torpedo planes were making their runs at water level. Some determined warrior had mounted a .30-caliber machine gun in a railing support just to starboard of the island, and when I heard it clattering away, I knew they must be really close. A bomb went off with a great flat bang that shook the ship deep in her bowels, where it had penetrated before the delay fuses fired. Then another big one, and the elevators jumped up in the air and came down, locked, with great bangs.

Then just up the passageway past the dive-bomber ready rooms near the admiral's quarters, there was a huge explosion. A bright red flame came like an express train down the passageway, knocking everything and everybody flat. A Japanese plane had crashed into the signal bridge and then ricocheted into and through the flight deck just forward of the area where we were sitting on the deck with our heads between our knees. Murph was grinning and gripping his cup of moosemilk tightly. The plane's bomb had rolled around and had not gone off, but its gas tanks had exploded.

Pursued by flames, we ran to the aft end of the passageway and up a ladder onto the flight deck at the aft end of the island. There the one-point-one gun crews were down in a bloody mess. Their magazines had been stacked in a circle behind them, and bullets from a strafing plane had caused them to fire at knee level into the gun tub.

We stood there debating whether to stay on the flight deck or take our chances below. Two great heavy thuds raised and then dropped the entire ship, all twenty thousand tons of it: torpedoes hitting home one after another on the starboard side—the death wounds of the ship, though we didn't know it at the time. The *Hornet,* turning at a sharp angle, shook like a dog shaking off water but immediately began to lose speed and list to starboard, which was terrifying, for you were still alive only so long as the speed was up and the ship was moving. You sense it in the soles of your feet, and it began to feel noticeably different at once, sluggish and dull, the rhythm off, and then another delay-fused bomb went through the flight deck just aft, through the hangar deck, to explode with a sharp sound somewhere deep below, followed by an acrid smell and smoke curling up out of a surprisingly small hole. The rudder was now jammed, and the ship began to turn in circles. The lights went out, and the fire hoses stopped putting water on the fires that now were everywhere.

The flight deck seemed too exposed, so we went down on the hangar deck, already listing sharply to starboard, with the edge of the deck in oily seawater running into the midships elevator pit. Then the forward bulkhead of the hangar deck exploded and the motor and cockpit of a burning Japanese plane crashed into the forward elevator pit. Its bomb also failed to explode, but its gasoline caught fire and the deck around the elevator began to glow. This plane had already done tremendous damage when it crashed into the gun sponsons on the bow of the ship, probably after the pilot was killed; or perhaps he was an early kamikaze, filled with battle will by the sight of the enemy ship so close and with the lust to obliterate it. One of the compartments he hit on his way through the bow was a blanket storage, and his plane had set the blankets afire and scattered them, burning and smoldering, the length of the hangar deck. Fine white blankets with blue bands—these were officers' blankets—and the smell of burning wool mixed with fuel oil remains my dominant sense impression of the day.

The guns stopped firing. The first strike was over, but by now the ship was dead in the water, and you had to be careful, so steep was the angle of the hangar deck, not to slide on the oily steel and out one of the openings and into the water on the starboard side, where the torpedoes had hit below the waterline, flooding the compartments below. The island and bridge hung menacingly out on the starboard side, seeming about to topple over and take the ship with them. There was fire forward where the plane had crashed into the elevator pit, and several bomb holes in the hangar deck were pouring out smoke. Among the burning and smoldering blankets dotted about were bodies, some terribly burned, others dismembered, some appearing unharmed. The burns were the worst, huge blisters oozing fluid, the tight, charred, smelly flesh, the member sometimes projecting as if straining for some final grotesque sexual act. A place not to linger, but there was now all-hands work to be done here. Damage control managed to correct the list somewhat, but power was still out, and firefighting had to go on by hand with buckets and a fire-retardant pow-der. The cruiser *Northampton* came up to tow the *Hornet,* sending over her steel towing cable to be attached to the anchor chain after the anchor was unshackled. The huge water-filled ship actually moved a bit, until the cable broke on the *Northampton* end and dropped in the water. There was no power on the *Hornet* capstan to haul it in, so it was dropped.

A second attempt was made using a two-inch steel cable that was stowed in the well of the midships elevator pit of the *Hornet,* a dark and slippery place by now, partly underwater. This cable, hundreds of feet long and tremendously heavy, had to be uncoiled and pulled, like some huge, stiff, greasy snake, by hand to the bow of the ship. Everyone in the area was rounded up for the job of getting the cable forward, and we formed a solid line up the hangar deck, slipping and sliding, heaving in rhythm, trying to move the dead weight of this metal boa constrictor. From time to time a single gun would go off, and everyone would drop the cable and take cover. But after a while we did manage to get the cable forward, and a sailor swam to the cruiser with a line to haul the cable across.

No planes would ever land or take off from the *Hornet* again, and the air divisions, my squadron included, provided free hands for the grim task of gathering the dead and wounded. I worked for a time on the flight deck helping to carry the injured crewmen from the gun mounts and the bridge to a corner on the high port side forward where the doctors had set up a hospital and rigged some awnings to protect the wounded from the brilliant sun that shone all day.

As I started back across the flight deck, the guns began firing again as a single dive-bomber made a run on us. I lay flat on the deck, covering as much of my body as possible with my tin hat, trying to work my way into it, and thinking for the first time that I was likely to die, and resenting it, feeling that at nineteen I really hadn't had a chance to do most of the things people do and vowing to do them if I survived. From that moment to this, life has seemed a gift—overtime, in a way—and all the more enjoyable for it. The bomb missed, and I ran to shelter in a compartment in the island where hundreds of other sweating, frightened men huddled behind thin steel bulkheads. By now the ship felt terribly heavy.

All this time the *Enterprise* had remained in the distance while hiding under a squall from the Japanese planes, but about noon she too came under attack. The antiaircraft shells made the sky black, and the ship twisted and turned, but in the end she caught three bombs, one of which killed my friends Whitey and Dallas in the chiefs' galley, but no torpedoes hit, and, patched up, she continued to operate her flight deck. Our strike groups, having heavily damaged but not sunk one of the Japanese carriers, *Shokaku*, were returning. The *Enterprise* would take her own planes aboard and as many of the *Hornet*'s as possible, but the others would have to land in the water, where their crews would be picked up by the destroyers serving as plane guards. The *Enterprise* picked up speed and moved away to the north. On her deck the pilots taking off were shown what became a famous message chalked on a board, "Proceed without *Hornet*." As she became smaller and then went hull down on the horizon, we turned, feeling very lonely, to the business of survival. Three destroyers moved in alongside us on the elevated port side, only a few yards away, with their masts and yards swaying wildly back and forth as they tried to maintain station in the swell while passing hoses over to fight the fires. The *Hornet* did not move at all, but the lighter destroyers, pitching and rolling, from time to time would crash against us with a terrible clang. Their rigging would catch in the catwalk and tear away when they rolled back, their radar and fire control battered and broken in the process.

Lines were passed across, and we began to pull the wounded over to a destroyer, some in wire stretchers, others sitting in a boatswain's chair. Speed was crucial: we expected to be attacked again, and the destroyer would cut loose if that happened. Men stood by the connecting lines with axes. Those of us on the lines pulling the chairs and stretchers over to the destroyer ran down the oily hangar deck with the line and then ran up again, hoping to God that we wouldn't slip and go crashing into some piece of ragged iron or go skidding out into the oily water coming in on the starboard side. Fires still burned forward, bodies lay around the deck, but there was no time or need to move them now. Below, the work went on to try to restore some power, but the Japanese aerial torpedoes were real killers, in contrast to our own inept weapons, and there were no flickering lights indicating that the dynamos were starting up again. The ship was now the business of the ship's crew, particularly the engineers and the damage-control groups, and having nothing to do the Airedales were assembled on that ghoulish hangar deck. I asked an officer if the smoking lamp was lit. He was naturally annoyed by the foolish request with the danger of fire everywhere, so he snarled that surely a sailor could go one day in his life without smoking. I muttered something about "What if it's the last day?" and got away with it in the pressure of the moment.

Things did not look good. We were probably going to abandon ship, so it was time to prepare. I could not bear to leave all those new guns that I had polished so nicely that morning, so I made my way up to the ordnance shack, picked one out, and put it in a sack, just in case. Encouraged by my own bravado and stupidly feeling no fear of the ship rolling over and sinking, I then did one of those foolish and dangerous things that young men are inclined to do. I made my way down through several hatches and dark decks to my locker. The water sloshed ominously on the low side of the compartment, but my locker was on the high, dry side of the ship. A pillowcase held my basic gear, including a suit of whites in case we went someplace where there was liberty, but a diary I had been keeping for some time—contrary to regulations—was reluctantly left behind. In a moment I was back on the hangar deck, the envy of all my friends for having salvaged some clothes, answering muster in preparation for going onto a destroyer.

About 1500 the destroyer USS *Hughes*, DD-410, stretched cargo nets between the two decks. The *Hornet* sat heavy and still, but the *Hughes* rolled and pitched wildly. When she came into the *Hornet* she crushed the net and anything in it between the sides of the two ships. Trial and error taught us the right way to do it. The trick was to jump just as the *Hughes* began to roll out, being careful that your foot landed on one of the tightening ropes, and not in the holes between, for there wasn't time to recover and make your way slowly up a loosening net. If you did it right you landed on the rope, and its stretch would pop you like a trampoline onto the deck of the *Hughes* and into the arms of several of her crew. Carrying my pillowcase filled with my contraband pistol and my liberty whites, I leaped for my life and made it with a great bound of exhilaration. Tricky, but better than going into the oily water where anything could go wrong.

At the best of times in war, a destroyer is a small and crowded ship, and as the wounded and about four hundred additional men squeezed aboard, every space above and below deck was filled to the point where it was difficult to move. Just after I got aboard, another Japanese strike, launched from their last operating carrier, roared in. The *Hughes* cut her lines, pulled away at high speed, and started firing her antiaircraft guns. Looking for a place with some protection, so solid with sailors was the deck that I crawled under the mount of the after five-inch gun, which swung around above me, the bolts holding the gun to the swiveling mount missing me by what seemed no more than a quarter of an inch. The firing directly above and the clang of the hot shell as it came out of the breech was too much for me, and I crawled out thinking what a real mess it was going to be if a plane came in strafing, with the deck absolutely filled with people who couldn't move without going over the side. In a moment one did, and I forced my way into an after deckhouse already crammed with sailors trying to cover up their heads. The enormous power the destroyer was turning up gave a speed of about forty knots and forced the stern deep into the water, forming a huge stern wave that made it impossible to see anything aft except a wall of water. The destroyer was not hit, but it seemed as though we were going to go down because some of the incoming Japanese torpedo planes made their run on the *Hornet* from behind the *Hughes*, zooming along on the wave tops and then juking up and down at the last moment. The carrier took more bombs and one additional torpedo, making her death certain. In the same attack the *Northampton*, trying to avoid a spread of torpedoes aimed at her, dropped the last towing cable, ending that slim hope of saving the *Hornet*.

The destroyer's officers began sorting us out, putting the injured below deck near the sick bay, arranging for each group of survivors on deck to appoint one man to come to the galley to draw food twice a day. The Torpedo 6 ordnance gang, about seven or eight of us, found ourselves aft on the starboard side, sitting on a narrow deck with our backs to the after deckhouse bulkhead and our feet outboard to the rail resting in the scupper. It was an uncomfortably wet place at high speed, but there was a rail welded to the bulkhead just above our heads to which it was possible to tie yourself, even when hanging onto a full pillowcase, which I began to curse but refused to give up. The very long day of October 26, which I always celebrate privately, was drawing toward sunset. We were circling the *Hornet*, but as it became clear that no power could be raised and that the effort to tow was finished, the command was given to abandon ship, and the crew began to go over the side on ropes and to jump into the oily waters. There was no room for any more survivors on the *Hughes*, so as the other ships moved in to pick up the rest of the crew, the *Hughes* turned south and began withdrawing. The Battle of Santa Cruz was over, and sitting on the deck, cold and exhausted, looking at the smoking carrier sitting there at an odd, lumpy angle, I considered for the first time the possibility that we might lose the war. The *Hornet* had been such a big and powerful ship, and yet only a few hits in a brief space of time had been enough to finish it.

But the navy would be back, and even in going down the *Hornet* was tougher than we thought. Later that evening our own destroyers went back to finish her off with their five-inch guns, but after several hundred rounds, they failed to put her down. By then the Japanese surface fleet was getting close—they were still trying to force their famous surface battle— and the American destroyers withdrew, leaving the scene of the battle and the hulk of the *Hornet* to the victors. She was too far gone to be salvaged, though, and a few Japanese long-lance torpedoes blew the bottom out of her during the night, and she went down in more than three miles of water to where she must still be sitting. It seemed the final irony that our torpedoes and guns couldn't even sink our own ship, that we needed the Japanese and their weapons to finally put it down.

SEVEN

Wandering

Murph must have been having ferocious withdrawal symptoms, for he sat all day with his ordnanceman's red-cloth helmet buckled under his chin, his brown, worry-sharpened face with its huge hooked nose looking out to sea like some naval muse of tragedy. It was my turn to go below and get the food for the ordnance gang, still on the deck, and Murphy, in one of his fits of wryness, gave me his chief's hat to wear, which he had carried with him, insisting that with it I could go to the head of the serving line. Since I looked about sixteen years old, in a navy where chiefs were still old and grizzled, it was an obvious joke, but I played my part to the hilt, crashing the line, giving abrupt orders about the corned beef sandwiches and coffee, and never dropping a smile. It must have amused others too because they let me get away with it, even asking admiring questions about how I had made chief at such a young age, to which I responded with tall tales of skill and daring against the enemy.

It took only one night on that exposed passageway on the ship's weather side, splashed all night by waves, to make it absolutely necessary to find some less exposed place on the crowded deck. Getting below was impossible. In the morning we began to scrunch forward to the well deck, where the torpedo tubes were located. A little pushing and shoving, some curses here and there, and we found some room under the inverted vee where the two flues from the boilers came up at an angle and joined about five feet above the deck to form the destroyer's single smokestack. The deck here was hot from the boilers beneath, which was fine for a time, and good for drying out, but it got too hot all too soon. We adapted by laying down cardboard and sleeping on it as long as we could take it, then climbing out to cool off by perching on the torpedo tubes for a time, and then diving back into the heat and sleep. Wherever you were you lashed yourself to something before going to sleep since waves washed over the deck from time to time. We were all pretty numb, which helped, and grateful to be alive under any conditions, which helped even more. But by the end of the fourth day we were just hanging on when the *Hughes* came to the entrance of the New Caledonia reef and took us to the anchorage off Nouméa.

Small craft took us off at once. Trucks met us in the dark, blackout being enforced, and bumped up the island to dump us at a tent camp where we were told to draw a folding army cot and mosquito net and find a place to sleep. Used to the insect-free life aboard ship, I didn't secure the mosquito nets properly, and by morning my feet were so swollen from bites that I couldn't get my shoes on. We were on a beach that backed on a salt marsh and some high, bare mountains. There was an Australian group, wonderfully jolly, camped on one side of us, and a New Zealand regiment, terribly dour, on the other, there to defend the island. Someone had decided that the nearly three thousand men from the *Hornet* would make dandy support troops if the Japanese invaded.

It seemed as if it might come to that one day when two barges were sighted by patrol craft and identified as Japanese carriers leading an invasion force. But fortunately the Japanese never got around to invading New Caledonia, and we passed our time swimming, gambling, and sneaking out over the mountains to pester farmers in isolated farmhouses—"Avez vous vin?" A few bottles of sour wine mixed with juice squeezed from the lemons growing all around us made for a wonderful party. We invited some Australians, and they filled us with stories about what stuffed shirts the New Zealanders were.

The *Hornet* crew was too well trained to be left on the beach for long in a time of shortage of trained personnel, and within a few days the ship's crew was sent off to the States for leave and reassignment. Air squadrons were needed in the ongoing struggle for Guadalcanal, however, and each of the four *Hornet* squadrons was divided in two. One group, made up of those who had been overseas longest, was sent home. The second group was used to form small new squadrons. Having been overseas only a year, I fell into the second group, and we all gathered around Murph, Moyle, Berto, and others to see them off on the trucks and tell them to have one for us in Dago.

The rest of us, a very young group, were reunited with six of our old pilots and given some new planes to form a small squadron to be sent up to the Canal, where the fighting got worse every day. Our flying field was an old colonial French racetrack, with a rickety wooden grandstand for quarters and workshops. It was a pleasant enough place, except that the wind blew dust over everything, including the guns and engines we had just worked on. But life in the grandstand, with its benches for beds and tables, was casual and relaxed, the weather warm and sunny, and we could wander into town whenever there was no work to be done, so long as we weren't out after sundown and curfew. It was nothing like the famous novel by James Michener and musical *South Pacific,* but island life was nice, and an occasional ride in a plane gave a view of a long island stretching out for a hundred miles, mountains down the center, white beaches, and a fine coral reef extending around the entire coast.

It didn't last long, though, and one night after sundown we were told to load the planes with all the spare equipment, pack our gear—there had been an issue of a survivors' kit—and go down to the dock where, at the end of the quiet Nouméan street, hundreds of sailors were lined up in the dark, out to the end of the wharf. The water was full of small squid, and in the kind of weird humor adopted by young men at war, the sailors on the edge of the dock would reach into the water, pick up a squid, and throw it up in the air to let it land on someone's head or face. For the victim, not knowing what the clammy thing was, standing tightly packed in absolute darkness and unable to move, already nervous and uncertain, it was real psychological torture, and the furious reactions came close to breaking out in a riot.

In time, excruciatingly slow time, small craft took us out to the USS *Kittyhawk*, a strange old tub used before the war for hauling boxcars loaded with bananas from Central America. The middle third of the main deck was open so that a crane could lower boxcars onto railroad tracks embedded in a cement deck, where they could then be rolled fore or aft. The *Kittyhawk* was now a plane transport, not a banana transport, and the decks were loaded with planes of all kind, including our own, destined for various islands. The ship was overloaded, and we slept on deck, getting under the upper deck when the rain squalls came, as they often did. Fine, but as we moved in among the planes looking for a place to sleep, dogs started snarling and barking frenziedly.

All along the outer bulkheads were chained German shepherds and Dobermans, the most ferocious bunch of dogs I have ever met. These were war dogs going to Guadalcanal to smell out Japanese soldiers—God help them—in the jungle. Their chains were short enough to keep these excitable creatures from getting at one another, but any human other than their handlers—who seemed to be hiding somewhere—who stumbled into their arc was in big trouble.

By daylight we were beginning to wallow along north between two chains of islands that formed the New Hebrides group, leading up from the south to Guadalcanal. It was rainy and steamy hot, and the islands, low and dark and close, had a look that made you vow not to go near them if you could help it. Food was hard to get in the crowded serving lines, and not worth it when you did, but you could buy candy ("pogey bait") at the ship's store, and a group of us bought a huge bag of small Hershey bars. A new member of the ordnance gang taught three of us to play whist—not bridge but old-fashioned, eighteenth-century whist—and we sat all day long playing, gambling, of course, eating chocolate bars and jumping at the sudden snap of canine teeth whenever the player sitting with his back to the dogs raised his hand and reached back to throw his winning card triumphantly down to take the trick. We agreed that the ace of clubs seemed particularly to excite them. Otherwise, the dogs sat looking at us rather coolly, while we avoided eye contact.

By the next day we were at Espíritu Santo, the largest and northernmost of the New Hebrides. Here we learned that our small torpedo squadron was not going to the Canal but, with a pickup group of fighters, would become the air group of an escort carrier, the USS *Nassau*, anchored off the island. The *Nassau* was one of the many small carriers that had been built in a hurry by adding a flight deck onto the hull of a large freighter, putting in one small elevator aft, rising from the hangar deck to the flight deck, and adding a tiny island about halfway forward on the starboard side for a bridge and air-control. Planes were launched by catapult, the deck not being long enough to fly off and the ship incapable of getting up enough speed to help out very much, twelve or thirteen knots being about tops.

After the great fleet carriers like the *Enterprise* and *Hornet*, the *Nassau* seemed small and dangerous. Our eyes lit at once on the torpedoes, warheads attached, locked in racks running up the side of the hangar deck, the only place aboard ship to put them, probably, but exposed to any accident or explosion. The *Nassau* and her type were not intended for carrier battles, but after the loss of the *Hornet* we were now down to one damaged carrier in the Pacific, the *Enterprise*. If the Japanese made an all-out assault on the Canal anything that could launch planes would be thrown into the battle, and so a few of these small and awkward carriers were backing up the front line. We might be able to surprise a Japanese fleet by coming from some unexpected direction. Once a plane gets in the air it doesn't matter where it came from, super carrier or the deck of a converted cargo ship.

It was a cramped ship, and the squadron was in no mood to make the best of it. We were naval snobs, used to the big ships and the smartness of the prewar navy, and everything about this little tub offended our sense of propriety. We sat around playing cards and bitching endlessly about everything aboard. At anchor the weather was stifling and the humidity overwhelming. We were crammed in a tiny compartment designed for half as many men, and the ship had no ship's store, barbershop, or "gedunk locker" (ice-cream counter). The food was dreadful.

Our planes—TBFs and fighter planes, the F4F Wildcats—were kept ashore on a muddy field where we went daily to work and to gossip with the army, navy, and marine pilots and crewmen who were flying into and out of the Canal daily. Guadalcanal came to have a mythic status as the place of death as stories were told along the flight line of desperate land battles just at the end of the runway mats on Henderson Field; of planes taking off and dropping their bombs almost immediately on Japanese ships coming down the Slot; of nighttime shellings by Japanese battleships; and of our own ships firing into one another in wild confusion during night battles. We ate it up, half longing to go to the mysterious place and half hoping to stay in reserve.

There was only waiting. Christmas and New Year's Day came and went. The natives were happy to climb a coconut tree and throw the nuts down and show us how to open them by putting a sharpened stick in the ground and driving the nut on it, which broke open the husk. But this amusement had its limits. Mail arrived, including Christmas packages sent months before, leaking melted soap and chocolate—everything melted on Espíritu Santo—smelling of after-shave lotion and writing paper. A huge mound of unopened packages belonging to the members of the squadron who had already gone home was piled up in a small compartment where it was raided by anyone in need of a razor or reading matter. Shaving lotion seemed to be in every package, and we were all wondrously fragrant, though we looked like a bunch of pirates.

The intelligence officer of the original squadron had been a notable pain in the ass, and one way of lifting flat spirits was to root through the deteriorating pile of Christmas packages until you found one—there were surprisingly many—addressed to Ensign B. and then to loot it, with many foul jokes about B.'s ancestors, person, and practices. I carried for years an ersatz pigskin toilet kit some loving aunt had sent him, and every time I used it I felt a modest revenge on a foolish but dangerous man who had threatened to have me shot for falling asleep leaning against a plane one night on the *Hornet* while I was standing guard over the planes on a closed and stifling hangar deck in a temperature over one hundred degrees, after working for more than twenty-four hours. "Ah, ha, Ensign B., you prick," a silent monologue would begin while I washed up in the morning, "you may be arising in some golden place from between the silky loins of your tawny-haired and adoring mistress to go have bacon and eggs with the admiral and dictate naval strategy, but I am enjoying the greater pleasure of taking my gear out of your fitted Florentine toilet kit with its watered-silk lining . . ." My feet would be submerged in several inches of soapy water, the sweat running into my eyes to the point where it was hard to shave, the smells of farts and shit from the group of straining men sitting on the open trough clogging my nostrils, some hairy, naked sailor letting lose a string of foul language—but taunting Ensign B. with newly imagined insults kept me happy and smiling.

By the end of January the Japanese assault in the Solomons had lost its sharpest edge, and they largely abandoned their efforts to supply and reinforce their troops, pulling back to Bougainville and to their base at Rabaul. The Japanese advance that had begun at Pearl Harbor had finally been halted. Our anchor came up, and we chugged eastward to a new anchorage off the northern coast of the main island of Fiji, where we were a threat on the flank of any Japanese warships coming down from Truk to the Solomons or the Coral Sea.

There was no port here, and so the ship was anchored, quite alone, offshore, surrounded by a torpedo net that retained the ship's garbage and the sewage from the heads quite efficiently. Uninviting, yes, but as the heat built up, swimming was allowed, and even the most fastidious went booming off the deck, trying to avoid the floating turds in the crystal clear water below. After a while, like many things, it didn't much matter; then the snakes arrived: some kind of white-and-black-striped coral snake that swam upright in the water, moving its tail back and forth in a most sinister fashion. There was debate about whether it was poisonous. No one really seemed to know for sure, but the swimming stopped.

A small group of us were sent ashore to service our planes, located at an army air base. We could eat in the mess hall there, but we seldom did, for it was a long walk—several miles—from where our tents were pitched in a grove of cool trees. There the natives soon found us and brought us sugar cane, coconuts, and pineapples fresh from the fields where they worked. The Fijian natives were noble, intensely black Melanesians, generous and with a fine sense of humor. They were also delighted to see us and to clean out the tents, wash clothes, provide fresh pineapple centers for breakfast, and take us at night to native dances in little one-room schoolhouses, where we sat on mats, joined in the songs, watched the intricate dances by men and women, and drank the local drink, kava, made from some pounded and fermented root. It seemed never to have any effect, but it gave you something to drink and encouraged a spirit of merriment. From time to time military police in jeeps would stop to make sure that no servicemen were mixing with the natives. A whistle from native lookouts would alert us, and we would run out into the fields to hide among the cane or pineapples until the police had left.

Strong loyalties were built up in a short time with the Fijians, involving the exchange of gifts: a woven mat for a pair of shorts or a Zippo cigarette lighter. From time to time we would go to the nearby town of Nandi, inhabited almost entirely by Indians, the descendants of the laborers who had been brought by the British to work in the fields in the late nineteenth century. By this time the Indians had become merchants, who beat silver coins into jewelry and ran small grocery and dry goods shops. The town was dusty and hot, and since we had little money, our pay records having gone down with the ship, we bought nothing with the small emergency pay that was given us. We identified with the Fijians, a carefree warrior people who delighted in filling us with stories about the wicked and unnatural ways of the Indians. We agreed happily, ate more pineapple, drank more kava, and sang endless verses of the Fijian song, "Ise lei, nona nogurawa," or something that I remember that way.

Occasionally, one of us would go back to the ship for a shower and to get cigarettes and candy bars, both of which the Fijians loved. On one of these errands I got caught for shore patrol. In the old days each ship's division took a turn furnishing shore patrolmen to keep order in liberty parties and to see that everyone got back aboard without wrecking anything. The idea was to take care of the men and protect the citizenry from them, not to assert authority. Still, not a popular job, but I was stuck, issued an SP brassard, a nightstick, a pair of canvas leggings, and a .45 automatic in a holster attached to a web belt buckled around the waist. Someone had discovered an old hotel up in the hills, about three miles from the shore up a steep red-dirt road, where cane whiskey was to be had. Worried about the crew going crazy from the heat and the boredom, the executive officer decided to let a liberty party go each day for a couple of hours to see the countryside and have a few drinks.

The day began badly, with a light rain, and worsened as the liberty boat came alongside, an old, battered fifty-foot motor launch ordinarily used for hauling garbage and not cleaned for its new purpose. In the heat, the smell went down into the stomach right away. Mustered on the hangar deck, the liberty party looked fine, as usual—brightly washed, carefully pressed whites; shiny black shoes; clean hats. No neckerchiefs required in this liberty port. Nothing looks more innocent or reassuring about human nature than sailors lined up to go on liberty. Few things look more depraved or less reassuring than when they return, and this liberty party was going to be a monumental demonstration of that truth.

There being no gangway, the sailors scampered smartly down a metal ladder that hung from the quarterdeck down to the motor launch below.

As the launch moved away toward the shore, the rain began to come down and bits of leftover garbage began to slosh around on the deck. There was no dock, so the launch ran aground, and the sailors jumped over the side and frolicked like clean white lambs up the road that was already beginning to turn to oozy red mud and wash into deep gullies. When the rain began to get serious and tropical, the brims of white hats were turned down to shed the downpour.

A large percentage of the old navy was alcoholic, getting blotto whenever they could, and we were driving some world-class sponges toward a long bar in an old wooden resort hotel that sold some of the rawest popskull on the planet. The first real drink after months of imbibing shaving lotion and paint strained through a loaf of bread relaxed them a bit. There was even some good-natured laughter, not the feral, drunken variety, here and there as one group stood under the leaking eaves while the others fought their way to the bar, a dollar a shot, and then new groups elbowed their way through. With the second drink people began to stand on their dignity, ancient quarrels broke forth in new mutinies, and hard words began to be heard. Intentionally, no officers had accompanied this fête, and the SPs had been told to head the gang back down the mountain when things began to get rough. That time arrived with the third drink, as fighting began right down in the mud, with kicks and eye gouging. The Fijian who ran the bar offered the SPs a free drink as we started back, and though it was absolutely against the rules, we knew we were going to need it and took it gratefully.

The sailors had to be forced away from the bar, and straggling, slipping, and falling they made their way cursing down the mountain, stopping from time to time to piss and fight a bit more. In the mud, rain, banana trees, and heavy foliage, discipline began to break down, and some of the squirrellier sailors began to roll in the mud and disappear into the jungle alongside the road. Where they were going, God alone knew. Back to nature, I thought, as, soaking with sweat and rain, I bird-dogged them through the underbrush, trying to keep them moving down the mountain. The SPs were like sheepdogs, fanned out in a semicircle at the rear keeping the flanks in and harrying everyone to keep moving.

In my sector a bitter, drunken black mess attendant started a quarrel with a sailor he cursed as "a dirty Jew." Why the black picked a fight with a quiet Jew rather than a redneck southern WASP, of whom there were many, was beyond me at the time. The old navy was covertly anti-Semitic and openly racist. There were many blacks in the navy, but they were segregated at that time in menial jobs as officers' mess attendants, cooks, and pantrymen. It was a lily-white navy that never gave its racism a thought, and I was about to get a lesson in its strange effects. The black was persistent and, crazed by the cane whiskey and a lot of accumulated frustrations, he kept tackling his victim and wrestling with him in the pouring rain. I separated them time and time again, only to find them once more down in the mud.

At last we got them to the launch, the rain still pouring, and the liberty party—covered with filth and mud, drunk and disorderly—put off from shore to go alongside the *Nassau*. Since there was only a swaying ladder up to the quarterdeck, where the august officer-of-the-deck in his freshly starched whites stood looking pained, getting the drunks to go up was a real problem. There is nothing a drunken sailor likes better than defying authority when returning from liberty. "Quarterdecking" was the standard term for acting a lot drunker and crazier than you were at these times. This particular scene offered lots of opportunities for quarterdecking: dropping off the ladder into the water, to be fished out with a boat hook by the boat crew, or vomiting as close to the officer-of-the-deck as possible.

But my two were the stars. We had separated them in the launch and kept them that way, sending the mess attendant up the ladder first. But as he got onto the deck, with me following hard after him, instead of turning aft and saluting the flag, with a wild cry he picked up the big wooden box in which liberty cards were deposited and, raising it high over his head, hurled it down the ladder at the Jew who by now was mad as hell himself and cursing down below in the boat. That finished it. The really tough master-at-arms who was on duty on the quarterdeck knocked the mess attendant down and hauled him off in an instant, lest his outstretched body offend the majesty of the navy. Those of us who were SPs that day were only amateur policemen, and we would not have reported the trouble at all, as long as we all got back in one piece, but the masters-at-arms had to be a rough sort, and their ability to keep the peace had been questioned in the full face of authority. I never heard what the punishment was, but I think it must have been awful.

Scuttlebutt began to say that we were going back to the States. The remnants of Air Group 6 were transferred, without planes, to another escort carrier, the *Copahee*. It seemed at first as though it could never happen, but sometime in late February the nets were taken away, the anchor came up, and the ship got under way for San Diego. No room anywhere, so we were given canvas army cots and set them up on the hangar deck. The galley served food all day long and we chowed down at odd hours. Somewhere south of Pago Pago, as we stared longingly at Samoa in the distance, some of the ship's boilers went off line. The already maddeningly slow standard speed of ten knots decreased at once, and the coast of California receded farther into the distance. The USS *Copahee* defined tedium: there on the vast Pacific, sun blazing down, nothing else in sight, the horizon unmoving, proceeding from Fiji to San Diego at six knots, clumping away. Trying to relieve the boredom I got into a poker game over my head, attempted to run a bluff on a card shark, and lost the pay I had finally received and saved for the thirty-day leave we would get in San Diego. Despair and ennui struggled for mastery, but a borrowed fifty cents got me into a penny-ante game made up of those who had lost everything in various bigger games run throughout the ship by the sharks putting together a stake for the fleshpots of America. A run of luck raised my capital to over eighty cents, fifty of which I used to buy a ticket in one of the anchor pools that various entrepreneurs were running.

In an anchor pool there are a set number of chances, each marked with a time. The winner is the owner of the chance marked with the exact time (always officially noted in the ship's log) that the pin is knocked out of the shackle to release the anchor chain, or, if the ship is tying up at a dock, that the monkey fist on the first heaving line strikes the dock. The pool I had bought into had 720 chances, one for each minute in a twelve-hour period—morning or afternoon made no difference—which meant that those who ran the pool had collected three hundred sixty dollars, of which they would give the winner three hundred, keeping a profit of sixty for their efforts. Fair enough, but with only one chance in 720, I forgot about it as the ship at last, in late March, came in sight of the coast, rounded Point Hard On, and worked up to a dock on the western end of North Island. As I looked at the naval training station across the channel, where I had arrived two years before, it seemed a lifetime away. The monkey fist sailed out in the air and landed with a clunk on the dock. The announcement "1024, first line across" came over the loudspeaker. The Airedales were to be transferred to some old buildings in the park at the San Diego Zoo, the other animals having gone somewhere else, and I had started off the ship when it hit me. I scrabbled to find my ticket, and there it was—"1024."

Pure delight! Good old Lady Luck had come through!. To get off ship, to go on leave, and to be rich, all at once. Three hundred dollars was a lot of money in those days, but now I had to move fast to make sure that I found the operators of the pool before they left the ship with all the money, or hid out somewhere down in the bilges until I was locked up in the zoo and couldn't get back. These and other dodges had been known, and all my suspicions were aroused, but the sailor who ran this pool was an honest man, hunting all over the ship for me, greeting me with real pleasure, and counting out the money in old, tired tens, fives, twos, and ones, a great wad I couldn't get in my wallet.

A happy, comic ending to a long, grim sixteen months of war, a real lift to the spirit, a feeling that things would work out.

EIGHT

Stateside

The desert sagebrush and mountains that had been so familiar two years before now seemed strange and bleak. The train was crowded, like everything else in the war, and as I looked out the window, I saw the cold March wind blow the snow ahead of it and the drifts lying here and there on the dry brown earth and the hard gray-green of the sage. I had expected my return home to be delightful, but the land seemed hostile after the tropics, and I was cold in my new set of tailor-made blues. My anchor-pool fortune had been partly spent on a Hamilton wristwatch, which I had always wanted—the last of prewar production still in the jewelry store—and a tightly fitted gabardine dress blue uniform: bell bottoms, zipper up the side of the skin-tight blouse, a dragon sewn in gold and green thread on the satin lining inside the front flap of the pants with their thirteen-button flap.

My leave had nearly ended in Union Station in Los Angeles. I had worn my issue dress blues with the loose blouse—we had been issued a full set of uniforms at San Diego—the bottom tied halfway up my chest and folded over to form a roomy pouch in which I had placed the .45 Colt automatic from the *Hornet* I was smuggling home. It was too risky, I thought, to put it in my sea bag, which was searched when I left the base, so along with a hundred rounds of ammunition—some tracer, some ball, some incendiary, the works: all for hunting rabbits!—it went into my blouse, making a grotesque lump. All went well until, in the middle of that huge waiting room, I bent over, and the gun, fully assembled, came sliding out the vee neck of the blouse, hitting the floor with an awful clang and sliding across the slippery surface at high speed. There were shore patrolmen all over the place, and visions of life in the naval prison at Mare Island flashed before my eyes. The SPs in the States at this time were ex-firemen and policemen, law-and-order types, not helpers like I had been in Fiji. Eye contact was enough to get you carded and patted down. I think that others must have seen the gun, but because it was the last thing anyone expected to see on the floor of Union Station, no one recognized it for what it was as, with what seemed nightmarish slowness, step by agonizing step, I ran after it, hunched over to conceal it, and slipped it back in my blouse.

The train pulled into Rawlins in the middle of the night, the temperature below zero, and we drove, my stepfather and I, the forty miles back to Saratoga, with nothing really to say, over the frozen land. By then—the middle of the war—most of the other young men were gone from the town, and I found myself the hero of the moment, invited to speak at the Lions Club on the progress of the war, as if I had any notion of how it was going; but I was flattered to be asked. The father of Bobby Mitwalsky, the marine who had been killed at Wake, broke down in tears and wanted me to explain why we had not gone to his son's rescue. I cried too and explained that we had wanted to, as if the crew had had something to say about it, but that it just hadn't been possible at that time; but we surely would win in the end and avenge old Bobby and his blue fur jacket. Everyone insisted on buying me drinks at the Rustic Bar, where I developed a taste for whiskey sours—it took months to get my stomach deacidified again—and a willingness to tell sea stories and talk naval strategy. All this lionizing was new to me—before the war I had not been one of the up-and-coming young men of even so small a town as Saratoga, Wyoming, population 680—but I took to the new role at once, casting off all restraints of modesty and good sense.

But it was the girls who really surprised me. My appeal to the girls in town had always been rather limited. I never had a regular girlfriend before the war and customarily had gone home after dances swearing never to go again and be humiliated by girls, plain as well as pretty, who found excuses to avoid dancing with me. In later years, my wife always said smugly, implying that she had been good enough to overlook this deficiency, "You looked too young." But in 1943 there were no other men in Saratoga, and the uniform really did, as I had heard rumored overseas, work magic. Girls who would never speak to me before were now willing to dally. Most myths are just that, myths, but the connection between sex and war must have some truth in it, for chastity seemed to have fled the Rocky Mountains to Alaska or some Arctic place, certainly not to California, for the duration. It was all terribly crude—awkward, drunken fumblings on car seats—but it was hot and full of life, joyously restorative and reassuring, a reminder that, even if clumsily managed, intense pleasure exists in a world that readily offers a lot of dullness and pain. Sex and war initiate us into society, and I began to feel more a part of what was really going on.

I even acquired a regular girlfriend—not very regular since I was in town for only a few days, but still in no time we were "going steady." Her name was Ruth Emery, and I was rather proud of the fact that she was several years older than my nineteen, a schoolteacher in the local grade school, but tongues wagged, and this was not good for her reputation in a small town where schoolteachers were watched by the local hawks for moral conduct. She seemed not to care; she was reckless and jaunty and independent, raised on a ranch near Valley City, North Dakota, with few illusions about life. But she had set her cap at me, and I was flattered. We agreed to be more or less engaged without any formalities and entered into a long, desultory relationship for the remainder of the war.

The past still threatened and could only be faced and then forgotten as much as possible. My mother's grave in the town cemetery on the dry hill overlooking the alkali lake just outside town was already collapsing and pocked with gopher holes. On one side, partly hidden by a rise, were the gray weather-beaten rodeo grounds, where men tried to tame beasts, and on the other was the town dump, spotted here and there with rusting cars from the twenties with unfamiliar names like White, Jordan, and Star. This was right, in the grotesque way life has of explaining what happens, for she was another discard from that era. Her family, Fletchers and Macmillans, lived for a hundred years on land in south Georgia distributed in land lotteries to Revolutionary War soldiers in the early 1800s when the Creeks and the Seminoles were resettled in Oklahoma. Life was rural: small farms, cotton and corn, Primitive Baptist churches, a few slaves until the Civil War, large families. The World War I generation to which she, born in 1900, belonged was the first to leave the land, and with a little education, she married a soldier, moved to town, went to Florida, lost the money from the sale of her father's farm in the land boom, had a child, divorced, and began wandering—Chicago, Memphis, a ranch in Wyoming.

She remarried, became a Catholic, and put a determined face on it all, but she was part of the first generation of really rootless modern Americans, moving restlessly by car about the country, emancipated socially and intellectually to a modest degree, but lost, really, without the supporting ethos and family that had protected people in the years when the continent was being settled. Alienation was the familiar state of my generation of Depression and another world war, but the old people had few defenses against it when it appeared.

People had changed in Saratoga, but not the land. The mountains were still there, as they will be for a long time. Streams of melted snow ran down from them to the Platte River, which ran down to the Missouri, which ran into the Mississippi and then to the Gulf of Mexico. I went up on one sunny day with a neighbor—Vernon Swanson, a crack shot

105

but not drafted because he had lost his trigger finger in a sawmill—to the ranch. The snow was still four feet deep down in the canyon, and we went on snowshoes, exhilarated by clear air and brilliant sun. The snow was melting, and the creek was running rapidly under the ice, giving that tinkle that comes with spring. Beyond the canyon walls the huge peak of Mount Vulcan loomed up above us, heavy and dark green, gradually blocking out the sun as we went farther up the canyon. By the time we reached the cabins of the ranch where I had grown up and my mother had killed herself, the sense of freedom and ease had gone, replaced by the heaviness of the mountains, cold snow, and gloomy pines. Indians avoided these mountains, and I think I know why.

At sea the war and its great battles had seemed more important than mere mountains and rivers, and I thought I had outgrown these pastoral scenes. But now nature reasserted its authority, reminding me of the durability and power that make human affairs, no matter how world-shaking, trivial and passing. The mountain in its unchanging sameness spoke too of nature's complete indifference to human ways of reckoning and feeling. Nature, it said, goes its way, and if humanity wants to tag along, fine, but our schemes and hopes do not affect the flows of nature.

Vernon and I drank whiskey from a clear pint bottle and then threw it up into the air, where it flashed in the light, turning over and over, and broke it with tracers from the salvaged .45. But this bravado only made us feel smaller, and after picking up the broken glass lest it harm some curious animal, we were glad to go down the canyon again, up on the ridge, and out of the shadow, if not the presence, of the mountain.

Thirty days' leave passes like all other time, and the transient barracks at the North Island naval air station was dark and noisy. A Texan in the bunk next to me kept a small rattlesnake that he had found out at the end of one of the runways and amused himself by putting on a glove and making the young snake rattle and strike. Terrified of snakes but ashamed to show how much, I was relieved when I moved to the torpedo squadron of a new Air Group 6 that was forming at North Island. Most of the members of the old squadron had been assigned to shore duty at the Assembly and Repair unit at North Island, but the new squadrons needed a core of veterans and, perhaps because I was younger than most, I was chosen to go back to sea. I was actually glad to join a combat unit again. There was something flat, even degrading, about life ashore: lying about your age to drink in cheap bars, sitting in dull movies, always broke and borrowing a dollar for liberty, shirking work, no sense of unity or purpose with the people you worked with.

Getting back to the squadron was different. Most of the new men were naval reserves who had joined the navy after Pearl Harbor, and they were socially and intellectually upscale from the old hands and the kids like me who had joined at the end of the Depression for lack of a job. There were a few old friends—Moyle was the chief of the ordnance gang. The new pilots and men were excited about going overseas and impressed by those of us who had already been there. McInerny was a hero to these newcomers. New squadrons are busy places, with an enormous amount of preparations for joining the fleet. For the ordnance gang this meant endless loading of practice bombs for mock bombing runs and rigging tow targets for gunnery practice.

One of the new sailors in the squadron was a man who became a close friend, Dick Boone. He later became quite famous as an actor, usually in villainous roles. He was several years older than I and had been educated at Stanford, but we hit it off, and he taught me a lot about the world, books, and art. I remember a small example, for some reason: his correction of my pronunciation of "Eyetalian" to "Italian." I went on several overnight liberties with him, riding the train to Los Angeles and staying with his family in Glendale.

It was the first I had seen of a well-to-do family and home. It was, I learned in time, as troubled as most, but I was overwhelmed by its comfortable ways. The Boones welcomed me warmly, and I soon fell madly in love with their seventeen-year-old daughter, Betty. This they did not welcome so warmly since in every way I was about as bad a prospect as a son-in-law as could be imagined. But their uneasiness never changed their kind attitude toward me. The father was a wealthy lawyer who had laid in a stock of fine whiskey at the beginning of the war. He was generous with it, and I thought it was the height of sophistication to ride the Sunday night train back with Dick from Los Angeles to San Diego at the end of a weekend liberty, drinking scotch—new to my palate— from a dimpled Haig and Haig Pinch bottle. Dick and I went to New York together after the war, sharing an apartment in the Village while I attended Columbia for a term and he went to the Neighborhood Playhouse, a famous method-acting school.

The war was moving on fast—new carriers, new squadrons—and by late May, Air Group 6, later commanded by Lt. Cdr. Edward "Butch" O'Hare, was loaded aboard ship and sent off to finish training on one of the Hawaiian Islands, Maui. O'Hare was a hero of the early war, having been awarded the Congressional Medal of Honor for downing five Japanese planes in one day when flying off the *Lexington* in the Rabaul raid in February 1942. His father had invented the mechanical rabbit chased by the greyhounds at dog races and was the victim of a sensational mob murder ordered, it would seem, by Al Capone. Chicago's O'Hare Airport was named for Butch O'Hare, who died at the end of 1943 in an incident in which I was to be closely involved.

We landed at Pearl Harbor and then, on a bright day with the wind blowing hard, went with all our gear onto a huge cement barge towed by a tug down past the leper colony on Molokai to land at Maui and the navy training field there. Most of Maui was brown and dry, and the field was built below the huge, bare, extinct volcano, Haleakala, that had formed the island. It dominated the landscape, and we often flew down into its dead crater, speckled with greenery. The airfield was rudimentary: short landing strips, earth revetments for the planes, wooden barracks. We were here to learn to work and fly together, and the days were long and busy. The nights, too, since night flying in formation was frequent, but somehow Maui still managed to seem like a tropical resort. The climate was perfect, sun and breeze, the discipline relaxed, and there was a beer garden, only a palm roof over a few rough board tables and benches, but we were allowed two bottles of beer a day, and they tasted like nectar at the end of a long hot day's work. We sat and talked, drinking the cold beer with the late afternoon breeze coming through the sides of the hut. I can remember Dick Boone telling us about life at Stanford, his fraternity doings avidly requested by us, and about his days as a prize-fighter and a painter in Carmel. Best of all he described how after his divorce he had overturned his Ford convertible, which his wife had preempted, when he saw it parked on the street with a big Saint Bernard in the back seat.

As always there was trouble in Paradise. Each of the officers got a bottle of whiskey a week, and one pilot who didn't drink gave a bottle to his radioman, Dutcher, who hoarded it in his locker and refused either to give us any or to drink it himself. This seemed downright inhuman and worthy of the most savage revenge. One night when Dutcher was in the air, we carried his locker out onto the field, where we shot the lock off and, leaving the locker there, took the bottle of whiskey to the empty beer hut and drank it with great satisfaction. Dutcher was extremely unpleasant about the whole business after he returned and found his locker missing, but he gradually came around and ended by saying that he only really minded that we hadn't saved him a drink, the bottle being empty by the time he found us. On another occasion word got around that one of the officers was keeping a kootch, a local whore with a tattoo of a mouse disappearing into her pubic hair, in a cabin down in the bushes, but that she was bored with the officer and wanted to meet virile young enlisted men. With a few beers inside us it seemed a fine idea for a jeepload of us to go down and visit her. She was less overjoyed to see us than we had been led to believe but was persuaded to show us her famous mouse, and in the end she was so pleased by our admiration that she dispensed favors to all, for a price. Whether she really had a relationship with any officer I never learned, but to think so made the experience somehow more satisfactory.

The skipper of the torpedo squadron was a fine man named John Phillips, who had enlisted in the navy back in the late 1920s in order to compete for an appointment to the Naval Academy. He graduated in 1933, getting his wings at Pensacola in 1936, and spent years as an instructor in instrument flying. This skill soon was to be of the utmost importance. One day he announced that he was looking for a new gunner. Moyle, loyal to the survivors of the *Hornet,* recommended me for the job, and after a few trial weeks I settled down to being the lead gunner in the squadron. No one minded, or even brought the matter up, but I had not a bit of training for the job. I knew about machine guns and had a general familiarity with planes, but of aerial gunnery—the deflection angles of two planes closing from different directions and speeds—I knew not a thing except what I had learned from hunting in Wyoming. But I was honored by the job, and it never occurred to me that there were skills in which I was dangerously deficient. But in those days we all picked up what we needed as we went along.

The lead gunner of the second division, flying with McInerny, was the fiercely mustached Buck Varner, former driver of the Los Angeles fire chief's car. I made bets on which division's turret guns would hit the tow-sleeve target most often. One day I persuaded Phillips to move in close to the sleeve and fly parallel with it at exactly the same speed. With this setup you couldn't miss, and the first division blew the target to pieces, leaving huge smears of red—the color of the paint on the tip of our bullets—on the ragged remnant of the target. Phillips stood laughing when we spread the first and second division targets on the tarmac in front of the ready shack. Buck Varner couldn't believe his eyes. For every hit his division had made, marked in black paint, on its target, there were fifty on ours. I played the game out for all it was worth but didn't take his money. Everyone had a beer, and the squadron laughed for days.

Like the old TBD, the TBF was a high-level bomber as well as a torpedo plane, equipped with one of the famous Norden bombsights of which it was always said, wrongly, that they could put a bomb in a pickle barrel from twenty thousand feet. Squadrons of Flying Fortresses had used them at Midway and not gotten a single hit on the Japanese ships. Each TBF gunner was also a bombardier, by virtue of his job, not his training. The radioman who sat down in the tunnel would get up in the turret while the gunner got down on the tunnel seat, opened the bomb-bay doors, turned on the sight in front of him, and looked down through a window in the bay to line up on a target far below. Only the lead plane of the division used the sight, while the other planes released their bombs when they saw the lead plane drop. The whole system, depending on variable winds and temperatures at different levels, was tricky, but I had a certain feel for the sight and great luck combining its functions with a lot of guesswork, raining down practice bombs on target on the bombing range.

The bombers practiced in a hangar, where an automated mobile box, looking something like a metal shoebox with wheels and a target pinned to the top, started from one corner. Riding a framework vehicle, steered by one man while the bomber sat about ten feet above and in front with the sight, you began a run on the slow-moving box. When your simulated bombing plane was directly above the target, you would release a plumb bob, the point of which, after a measured delay, would make a mark in the target. Like everything we did, this exercise was made more interesting by wagering on it. The mark closest to center collected the pool for the day. Boone wept and swore that I cheated, but day after day I walked away with the loot, acquiring a reputation as a master bomber, which I never tested in action since it must have been obvious to the admirals that high-level bombing with torpedo planes was a waste of time. We had the sights only because the army had them and the navy didn't want to be left behind.

The plane's crew's relationship with Lieutenant Commander Phillips was formal. The radioman—a telephone lineman from Reno named Sullivan, short enough to stand upright in the tunnel—and I called him captain, and we asked permission to fire the guns and secure the hatches as if we were on a battleship. But Phillips was a genial man, given to taking off for the day to have lunch in Honolulu or to fly over the great volcano on the main island of Hawaii, landing at the little Somerset Maugham tropical town of Hilo, where we would wander about while he borrowed a jeep and toured the island. On the way to Honolulu we never missed a chance to fly low over the leper colony on the long spit of land with the cliff at the end on Molokai, and the lepers never failed to come out, either to wave or to shake their fists at us; we never knew which.

There were endless training missions in which the squadron took off, assembled, flew to a target together, bombed it, and then formed up again and flew home. Woe be to the pilot who didn't join the group quickly or fly a tight formation. One poor fellow, known as Dilbert after a cartoon character used in flight training posters who did everything wrong, spent an hour one bright moonlit night trying to find the seventeen other planes of the squadron as we flew back and forth over the great dead volcano. Finally, Phillips had had it and after asking Dilbert for his location, told him to stay right there and we would join up on him. We did, and Ensign Dilbert went back to the pool the next day for further training.

Wyoming snow: on the way to the navy,
age seventeen, winter 1941

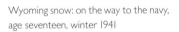

Main Street, Saratoga, Wyoming: pop. 650,
ca. 1933

Frank and Kate Kernan, stepfather and
mother, 1937

Paul Cadmus, "The Fleet's In," 1934, oil on canvas, Navy Art Gallery, Washington, D.C., 34-5-A

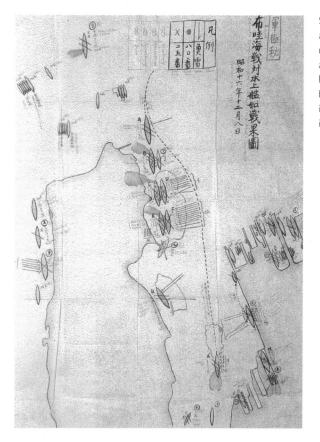

Sketch of the Japanese attack on Pearl Harbor, made by the Japanese air commander, Mitsuo Fuchida, for Emperor Hirohito. Parallel lines indicate torpedoes; "X" indicates a hit.

Slow, steady, and low: Torpedo 6, Douglas Devastator, TBD, the Midway torpedo plane, dropping a tin fish.

TBF-I: the Grumman Avenger, a new torpedo plane used after Midway

USS *Hornet*, under air attack and sinking at the Battle of Santa Cruz, October, 26, 1942

On leave, March 1943, wearing the new tailor-made uniform bought with my anchor-pool winnings

The schoolmarm: Ruth Emery, a romance that never bloomed

Dick Boone (*Have Gun, Will Travel*), Jim Gaffney, me, and Ed Dutcher in a San Diego bar, 1943

Ed Sullivan's elevator-cable splice, Butaritari, Gilbert Islands, 1943

Night-fighter radar plane crew: me, Hazen Rand, Ed Sullivan (on wing), and Lt. Cdr. John Phillips

Lt. Cdr. Edward H. "Butch" O'Hare, Congressional Medal of Honor, 1943

Overboard: Ens. Robert Dyer, me, and Moon Mullins after crashing off the catapult of USS *Suwannee*, 1945

Recreation at Mog Mog, Ulithi Atoll, 1945

Free beer: Torpedo 40 in Guadalcanal, 1945

Torpedo 40 aircrew: Mullins, Dyer, and me

Chief Petty Officer Kernan back from the war before my discharge

Much later, talking to the brass: my wife, Suzanne, and me with Adm. Jay L. Johnson, CNO, 1997

NINE

Black Panthers

By late October the idyll was over. The USS *Lexington* (CV-16), a new carrier replacing the old *Lexington* (which was lost in the Coral Sea the previous May), was cruising off the coast, and we flew out to her, practicing from her deck for several days. Returning to Maui, we packed up our gear, stuffed it in the planes, and flew to Ford Island. Pearl Harbor was filled with ships, and as we landed we saw several of the new carriers joining the fleet. The losses of the first year of the war had been made good, and the great drive across the central Pacific that would end in Tokyo Bay less than two years later was beginning. On November 10, Air Group 6 flew out to the *Enterprise* to prepare for an attack on the Japanese bases on the Gilbert Islands at the end of November. After we had landed aboard, the yeoman handed me orders directing me to report to San Francisco for training as a pilot. I had applied in Maui, having always wanted to fly, but had expected nothing to come of the brief physical and written exams I took. Now the orders were there, but there was no way to report until the cruise was over. I would go through the most remarkable events of my life during the next month with the constant thought that if the orders had come one day earlier I would have missed it all.

A huge task force of carriers, cruisers, destroyers, and transports sailed down the central Pacific to the Gilbert Islands, where we were to land troops on Betio (or Tarawa), with its landing field, and, slightly to the north, Butaritari Island in Makin Atoll. The *Enterprise* was assigned to provide air support for the army's Butaritari landing. The marines were to take Tarawa. Both islands were pounded with naval gunfire, and on the morning of November 20 the transports loaded the troops into the assault boats. Carrier planes went in to clean up any targets still standing and provide close support throughout the day.

Makin Atoll was Hollywood perfect: blue water, circular coral reef, white beaches, and coconut palm groves. We in Phillips's plane could see the entire show, flying liaison back and forth not far above the landing and reporting the progress of the assault to the command ship. Tarawa was a bloody mess from the beginning, when the assault boats hung up on the reef, but at Butaritari the attack proceeded like an exercise. The cruisers and destroyers blasted away, squadron after squadron of planes flew in strafing and dropping bombs, a long line of Higgins boats moved up to the southern hammerhead of the island. As the first soldiers rushed up the beach, hundreds of cheering natives rose up out of the recently shelled brush and broken trees and rushed down to greet them with open arms. The Japanese garrison had retreated earlier up the handle of the island, but the natives had stayed behind, eager to see Americans and be rid of the Japanese. It had been assumed that nothing could live through the pounding the assault area had taken, but few of the natives were hurt, and they gave a comic turn to the landing.

Later in the day we circled the island and observed a group of torpedo bombers try to skip bomb a wrecked ship half out of the water near On Chong's Wharf. The wharf, built years ago by a Chinese trader, was a wobbly structure sticking out into the lagoon and was about the only thing with a name on the atoll. A coastal trader that had sunk off it in some long-forgotten storm had been occupied by the Japanese, who were using it as a pillbox from which to fire at our soldiers after they had landed with their supplies on the beach.

Skip bombing was a new and briefly used technique in which you didn't try to hit the target directly but came in on a line with it, about a hundred feet above the water, and dropped the bomb at an angle so that it hit the water and then skipped up in the air and landed on the target. Bang! Utter destruction! Why this was thought a better way of destroying the target than hitting it directly was no more obvious than why two-thousand-pound armor-piercing shells designed for World War I battleships had been converted to skip bombs by installing fins and delay-action fuses. But they had, and they were being used that day on a rusty old wreck that you could kick a hole through. As we circled, eyes fastened on the spectacle, plane after plane came in, dropped its bomb in the sparkling clear water, only to have it hit the shallow sandy bottom, leap up, and skip over the ship to land with a big explosion on the beach side, or skip high up in the air and explode with a flash that threatened the plane that had just dropped it.

It was an exercise in the kind of dangerous futility that wars are made of. As we turned in a wide circle over the island, feeling smugly superior to the skip bombers, there was a ping, only a little one, and a smell of gasoline. It was trickling into the tunnel where Sullivan and an observer, the squadron intelligence officer, were seated. The bomb bay had been filled that day with a huge auxiliary gas tank to allow us to fly liaison all day without having to land to refuel. The auxiliary tank had no self-sealing lining, and when an irritated Japanese gunner took a shot at us, flying slowly, and no doubt infuriatingly, overhead, a lucky hit pierced the tank and the forward bulkhead of the tunnel. The plane filled with fumes that could explode with a single spark. The intelligence officer later wrote himself into the dispatches with a recommendation for a medal for himself—which Phillips did not forward—for saving the plane by pouring coffee from his thermos on the gas, thus, he said, holding down the fumes and preventing an explosion. Fortunately, no one was smoking at the time, and the pilot dropped the big green auxiliary tank on the Japanese lines, hoping that we hit the soldier who had hit us. The gas in the plane evaporated quickly and, nearly out of fuel, we flew back to the *Enterprise* to land, refuel, and take off, without our coffee-pouring intelligence officer, for another afternoon of observing.

There was little resistance on Butaritari, in contrast to the blood being spilled a few miles to the south in the terrible fighting on Tarawa. But the army advanced cautiously, and we flew far ahead of the troops, a few hundred feet above the blue water and the sandy beaches, weaving in and out across the reef and the island, looking for any signs of Japanese support troops or new entrenchments. Mostly we saw only natives, who waved happily. But as we flew back to On Chong's Wharf a Japanese soldier let rip with his machine gun, blowing some pieces off the plane, which then went into a dive that dropped my stomach right out of my belly. "Prepare to crash, prepare to crash," Phillips shouted over the intercom, and then the plane lifted a little. "I think I can hold it with the tabs." The tabs are small inserts in the elevator, controlled separately, that can be rolled up or down to keep the plane in a climb or descent without the pilot having to maintain constant pressure on the elevators. Now they compensated for the down pressure on the loose elevators and kept us in something like steady flight.

A bullet had come through the fuselage in back of the radioman and cut the steel wire elevator control cable that connects the pilot's stick to the elevators. We were okay for the moment, holding flying altitude not far above the water, but the problem had not been solved. Landing on a carrier is tricky business, requiring drumhead-tight control cables for hair-trigger responses. So it looked like a water landing alongside the carrier was the best we could hope for, and such landings, while they often worked, were always highly risky, particularly with faulty controls. Too many things to go wrong: a bump on the head, a jammed hatch, and the plane sinks instantly.

Radioman Sullivan got on the intercom to say that, using his telephone linesman's skills, he thought he could join the two raveled ends of the elevator control cable, which he proceeded to do, standing up in the tunnel below the opening of my gun turret, through which I looked down between my legs with great interest. A lot of time passed, with everyone literally sweating through their khaki flight suits, but finally the splice was made, and though the cable still had a lot of slack, Phillips could make the plane go up and down again using his stick. But that, he explained over the intercom, wasn't good enough for any kind of landing, on the water or the deck. The cable had to be taut and respond more or less instantly to his control. Sullivan, a little over five feet tall and able to walk upright in the tunnel, was a very ingenious and a very courageous fellow, and he said that he thought he could work some cord we were carrying into both sides of the splice and then twist a .50-caliber bullet into the weave and by turning it again and again, as in a tourniquet, take up a lot of the slack. This too worked after a long time, and Phillips finally declared himself willing to try a deck landing on the *Enterprise*.

The crew on the *Enterprise* was less sure. They didn't want the flight deck fouled with a wreck at that point, and though they finally agreed, they made us wait for another eternity, during which time Phillips tried out an idea on Sullivan. "What I am going to need at certain points in the approach and landing is a lot of movement in a hurry, and the patched cable will move the elevator too slowly. On the landing approach, could you stand in the tunnel, holding onto the bullet providing the tension in the cable, and when I say 'NOW' over the intercom, give the cable an instant manual assist in whichever direction it's moving?" Landing on a carrier is rough at the best of times, requiring the crew to be seated and buckled up; but Sullivan agreed to try.

Phillips was a master carrier pilot, and he flew the crippled plane carefully on a lurching approach. Every movement was slow and exaggerated and likely to lead to disaster. Sullivan hung on to the bullet for dear life, locked his feet on whatever he could get for purchase, and in the end, when Phillips said the final "NOW," pulled the cable with all his might to stall the plane out and drop it on deck, getting thrown into his radio as the arresting wire caught the tailhook and the plane stopped short.

November 20 had been an exhaustingly long day, long enough by far, but that night a formation of Japanese bombers flew down from the Marshall Islands to the north to look for our carriers in the darkness. They didn't find us that night, but we were at general quarters, all lights extinguished, for a good part of the time. This was not the only danger. I was sitting on the flight deck, my legs hanging over into the catwalk, when in the complicated maneuvering another carrier cruising with us rushed straight at us, a huge black mass, only to turn at what seemed the last moment and pass by us to port, so close that I could actually call out to the sailors standing helplessly on her deck.

The Japanese had big airfields on the islands in Kwajalein Atoll several hundred miles to the north, out of which they were flying two-engine medium bombers, Bettys, loaded with torpedoes, at the American fleet, hoping to sink a carrier or two. Japanese air losses in the Solomons had been so great in 1943 that they had turned largely to medium-bomber night attacks with torpedoes, flying at wave height to escape radar detection. Our ships were almost helpless in the face of these attacks, for we had as yet no night fighters, and if antiaircraft was fired it would reveal our position. It was decided on the *Enterprise* to do something about the problem, and Adm. Arthur Radford, commanding Task Force 50.2, consulted with Butch O'Hare and Phillips about setting up the first night-fighter operation off carriers, code-named "Black Panther." We had just received our first small airborne radar sets, ASB-1. They were primitive instruments, with a small green screen, about five by seven inches, with a moving arm that briefly lit up bogies as it swept across their location— terribly difficult to read—with a maximum range of about ten miles, and precise only at a much closer range. The operator had to switch from the aerial under one wing to the one under the other to see that side of his circle. Still, we had seen nothing like them before, so they impressed us mightily. Sets had been installed in two of our torpedo planes by a specialist, Lt. (jg) Hazen Rand, who had worked in the development of the airborne naval radar at MIT. After a crash course in operating the rear stinger gun, Rand replaced Sullivan in our tunnel for the Black Panther operation.

The night-fighter plan was straightforward: two radar-equipped TBFs with belly tanks would be launched at dusk to stay up all night. Then, when the bogies appeared later at night, as they usually did, fighters would be launched from the *Enterprise* and join up with the torpedo planes. The ship's fighter director officer (FDO), using the ship's radar and the VHF (Very High Frequency) radio, which the Japanese, it was thought, could not pick up, would vector fighters and a torpedo plane to a point near the bogies. There the more lightly gunned TBF, using its radar, would lead the two heavily armed fighter planes (six wing-mounted .50 calibers each) to where they could see the exhausts of the Japanese planes, which did not have exhaust suppressors at that time, and then break away, leaving the fighters to complete the attack. All could then land at daybreak, avoiding a night landing and the necessity of lighting up the ship, revealing its location to any enemy planes still hunting it.

The plan was modified as time passed, and when bogies appeared in large numbers on the ship's radar screen early on the morning of November 24, two night-fighter groups, each consisting of a torpedo plane— without the belly tanks, thankfully—and two fighters, were catapulted at about 0300. The second TBF was piloted by Lt. John McInerny with Buck Varner in the turret and another radar specialist in the tunnel. It was a confusing flight. We never joined up effectively, and when we did get into a kind of loose formation, the ship's radar couldn't get us in an attack position on the Bettys. Our plane radar found nothing. It was a long night, nearly six hours, of straggling around a dark sky without much sense of where we were and where to go. At about 0500, while we were circling looking for targets, there was a huge flash of light off to the east, like the sun rising, which we later learned was the escort carrier *Liscombe Bay* blowing up after being hit by a Japanese submarine torpedo. She was a small ship with pitifully little protection, and everything in her—gasoline, bombs, torpedoes—blew up all at once. She went down instantly, with the loss of over six hundred men. Our fears about her sister ship, the *Nassau,* when we first saw her at Espíritu Santo had not been exaggerated. Mac's plane developed engine trouble, but he nursed it through the night until he had to land after dawn with only five gallons of gas left in his tanks. The rest of us, disappointed, finally got back aboard about 0830.

The next day, the battle being pretty much over at Makin, we flew down to Tarawa with O'Hare to familiarize ourselves with the field so that we could land there after a Black Panther flight to avoid making the ship illuminate for a landing. A landing on a totally dark deck was still not conceivable. The fight was still going on in the midst of smoldering devastation. The landing field was clear—though it had a lot of holes and no landing lights—but the burned and gutted landing craft were still on the reef far from shore where they had hung up; the marines had gotten out with their weapons and waded ashore in neck-deep water. The bodies still floated in the tide and lay bloated on the sand. All the trees on the island were down in great rubbish heaps.

Early on the night of the 25th the usual flight of Bettys appeared early, but the Black Panthers sat the evening out. If we had launched at that time we would have had to land on Tarawa, and it was clear from the day's inspection that a night landing was out of the question. One snooper passed a few hundred feet over the ship—he may have dropped a torpedo—so close we could see his exhausts, but the *Enterprise* did not open fire so as not to reveal our position. This was all spooky stuff, and the Japanese made it spookier by dropping bright flares and yellow float lights here and there in the darkness, apparently to mark targets and assembly points. With all this going on the crew was nervous and jumpy.

One man began shouting at me that it was the duty of the Panthers to be up there in the night defending the ship, which seemed after the past hairy week very unreasonable. Let him go up there and defend the ship is pretty much what I told him, and a brief fight bled off a lot of repressed feelings.

Other Bettys circled from about twenty miles, dropping another string of flares. When they came closer, the battleship *North Carolina* and other escort ships opened up with antiaircraft guns in a startling explosion and shot down one, possibly two, snoopers. The night went on at general quarters as one or another group of bombers made a move on us and then withdrew to circle about confusedly, dropping more of those ghastly float lights just when you thought they might have gone away. No one got much sleep until the attackers left before dawn, with no hits to show for their effort.

For the night of the 26th another modified night-fighting scheme was designed, using only one section of a torpedo plane and two fighters going out together. One of the fighters was to be flown by Butch O'Hare and the other by his wingman from Fighting Squadron 2 (VF-2), Ens. Warren Skon. Phillips was to fly the torpedo plane with Rand in the tunnel, while I remained, somewhat unsure about all this, in the turret. I often thought that once you got in there and had pulled up the armor plate (wondering what "Hard Homo" meant), you were committed, and whatever happened, there wasn't much you could do about it. Infantry could turn tail at any time, but you were literally and figuratively locked in once you got into the confined space of the turret. This night would prove that theory.

The fighters were to go off the catapult first, followed by the torpedo plane, early in the evening, if the Japanese appeared. Then we would all have to land on the carrier deck in darkness, without lights. The secured landing field at Tarawa had been notified to receive us if we could not get back aboard the carrier, but no one wanted to risk landing on that field in the dark. Once in the air the plan was for the fighters to rendezvous immediately with the torpedo plane and use its radar eye, along with the ship's radar, to get close to the attackers.

Japanese snoopers were already probing the fleet before sunset, and daylight fighters from the *Belleau Wood* shot down one Betty. We Panthers sat in the ready room, wearing red goggles to preserve our night vision. I had no more than the usual worries, but waiting was hard.

About 1800, at dusk, the public address system told us that thirty to forty Bettys closing on the ships had been picked up by radar. A few moments later came that stirring command, "Pilots, man your planes," and the two fighter pilots, Phillips, Rand, and I made our way up to the flight deck and into our planes. Off to starboard three to five miles a string of red flares went off. Why red? I had checked and double-checked all the guns on the torpedo plane: the .30 caliber in the tunnel, the two fifties in the wings, and especially the .50-caliber Browning machine gun in the turret, making sure that the two one-hundred-round cans of ammunition I had—one in the gun, and one secured to the bulkhead below in the tunnel—were fully loaded with perfectly belted ammunition so that there would be no jams at a bad time. The belts for the turret gun were heavy with tracer—one tracer, one armor piercing, one tracer, one incendiary—so that I could see more clearly where the stream of fire was going in the night. A great mistake, it turned out, since too many tracers igniting at the muzzle of the gun blinded me in the darkness. In the turret I checked the intercom, pulled up the armor plate that locked me in with an ominous click, and turned on the hooded gun sight with its lighted orange concentric circles, just behind the bulletproof plateglass in front of me, while the engine turned up and went to full power.

The two fighters went off at 1800, fired from the catapult, and disappeared into the distance, diminishing blue lights visible from their exhaust flares, which could not be suppressed without loss of power. The TBF did have its exhausts covered and so remained invisible until we began firing. The FDO (fighter director officer) seated in the air control on the *Enterprise* vectored the fighters out toward the Bettys at once without waiting for the TBF to join them, a change in the plan that would have serious consequences. Torpedo planes always sank below the deck when fired from the catapult, and looking from the backward-facing turret, I could see the huge black deck rise above us and feel the tug of the waves below. But the engine at full power pulled us up and away, and as the wheels and flaps came up we gained altitude and began to move away from the white wakes and bow waves of the task force. The sun set a few minutes later, and the moonless night was completely dark, unlike the moonlit nights we had practiced in at Maui. An overcast began at about 1,500 feet. We expected the fighters to join up with us at once, but they were long gone, and we began a fruitless search for them, feeling annoyed and abandoned since we believed that all our firepower was in the fighters. Although nothing was said I suspected that Butch was looking for glory again.

Though we followed the vectors called out by the FDO trying to bring the planes together, we couldn't catch up with the fighters. I assumed that we had lost them for good and would go back to try to land on the ship. But Phillips was an aggressive pilot, and after a time he decided to see what he could find in the darkness on his own. Rand called out that he had a contact at seven miles and took us in to 4,500 yards before we lost contact. Shortly after 1900 our ships, except for the carriers, opened up with their antiaircraft guns, illuminating the horizon for us in an incredible *son et lumière* show. Still more flares were dropped by the Japanese, lighting up the ships like daylight for a few moments. When the flares burned out all was darkness again, and I found myself in difficulty. The pilot has instruments, particularly an artificial horizon, to tell him whether he is flying level or not, and an altimeter to show whether he is climbing or diving and how far he is above the ocean. The man in the tunnel doesn't care what is going on outside since he is enclosed in a box, oriented by his green radar screen. But in the turret, riding backward, you have no instruments. You stare out into the dark night, and after a time you don't know up from down. The first few turns are okay, but then disorientation begins. A flicker of light could be a star in the sky or a ship on the ocean or another plane coming at you on a fast angle. As long as the changes are not too abrupt and frequent, the seat of your pants gives you a sense of where you are, but a few rapid changes and panic begins to flutter around the edges.

The *Enterprise* radar was still trying to direct both the fighters and the torpedo plane to groups of Bettys, but Phillips was better at the game than O'Hare. He found himself a few miles behind a group of six, and Rand began calling out the range: three miles, two, one, a thousand yards. Then, at two hundred yards, seeing the Bettys' exhausts, Phillips said, "I have them in sight. Attacking." This was unheard of, a lightly armed, clumsy, relatively slow torpedo plane attacking several bombers in a tight, mutually supporting formation, each with five guns—front, rear, top, and two in the waist—but there was no call for a vote, and Phillip swung in behind the rear Betty in the starboard line.

The two .50 calibers in the wings felt like they were tearing the plane apart. As we pulled up and away from the firing run, I could look back and see the surprised enemy opening up with the guns he could bring to bear. Fire flared out at his wing root, where the gas tanks were, and I fired at the flames. He blew up all at once. A long trail of fire went down and down into the blackness of the ocean below, where it kept on burning, a red smear on the black water. The turret .50 caliber, its muzzle less than three feet from my eyes, spewed a flare of burning gases, despite a flash suppressor—all the more for the extra tracer, which in the darkness made it impossible for me to see the illuminated concentric circles of the gun sight. As long as I was seated I was blinded every time I fired. The only thing to do was to unbuckle my safety belt and crouch on my seat, trying to get my eyes high enough to see over the muzzle flare and fire down the line of tracer into the Bettys, illuminated by their firing guns and engine exhausts. It didn't work very well—I still could hardly see—but it worked a little bit, and I remained in that crouched position, my head bent over and forward to fit inside the rounded turret, for the remainder of the flight, except for the trip into the tunnel below.

The Japanese were totally confused. Night fighters from carriers were as unknown to them as they were new to us, and in their excitement the Japanese gunners were firing at one another. As we pulled away from the first kill, the fighter director officer vectored us toward other Bettys, and our own radar once again brought us to within visual range of the dark cigar shapes, their exhaust flares burning blue on both sides. Just as we went into our firing run, O'Hare, who had seen the first plane burning on the water, called us and ordered Phillips to turn on his recognition light so that they could join up: "Turn on your lights, Phil, I'm going to start shooting." The words filled me with terror. The fighters hadn't been able to find anything all night, and now out of the darkness one of the navy's aces was going to start shooting! To tense things up a bit more, Butch added, "I think I got me a Jap." Phillips, cool as ever, replied that he was in a firing run and did not want to alert the enemy but that he would blink a light a few times.

The light told the Betty that something was out there, and it began evasive maneuvers, opening up on us as it did so, but Phillips followed closely, and after a long burst the deadly fire showed again in the gas tanks where the wings joined the fuselage. I poured in some more, and the Betty started down in a controlled dive, making a long water landing, leaving a trail of burning gas about three hundred yards on the water and continuing to burn. I snapped off a burst at another dark cigar shape, and then Rand called out on the intercom, "I'm hit."

"Where?"

"In the foot. My boot has filled with blood. I don't know how bad it is, but I have put a tourniquet above the ankle."

"Are you in pain?"

"Yes."

"Too much to go on working the radar?"

"I don't know. I'll try."

"Kernan, go down and see what you can do."

I unlatched the armor plate below me and crawled down in the bucketing plane to sit on the green aluminum bench beside Rand. His pale thin face looked like a skull in the ghoulish green light of the radar screen. A single bullet had come through the plane just forward of the armor on the floor, where his foot was braced while he peered into the radar scope, and it had torn off the side of his shoe and foot. It wasn't a mortal wound, unless he bled to death, but it looked a painful mess. I put on a bandage and called Phillips on the intercom. "Shall I give him an injection of morphine, Captain?" (We carried Syrettes in the medical kit.) The answer shocked me. "No, we'll need the radar again." The logic was obvious, though I didn't think Rand was going to do much more work that night.

I took the opportunity of being in the tunnel to change the ammunition can for the turret gun, a tough job trying to shove a long heavy can up one minute and pull it down the next while hunched over in close quarters, the plane rising and falling rapidly. Each time I would get it nearly up to where the retaining latch could catch it, the plane would suddenly rise, and the can and I would come down to the deck or be flung against one of the bulkheads, trying all the time not to step on Rand, sitting there with his teeth gritted tight, or to slip in his blood. Finally the ammo can clicked into place, and I jumped back into the turret, glad to get out of the dark and bloody tunnel. We had by this time lost the Japanese planes, but Phillips, true to form, began searching for them again. The radar was our only chance, but now Rand could pick up no blips in any direction. He was making heavy going of it by that time, though trying gamely. We were now circling at some distance from the carrier, and I became disoriented again. The second of the two Bettys that had crashed was burning in a long smear of gasoline on the water, and as we turned in the pitch black, I thought the ocean was the sky and the light from the burning plane another plane turning in a long curve for a run on us. I called out on the intercom that it was attacking and requested permission—this was still the battleship navy—to begin firing. Phillips put me right side up again.

The ship's radar could see both us and the fighters, and the fighter director officer was still trying to maneuver us together. At this point Phillips turned on all our running lights, and the fighters, lit up like Christmas trees, slid menacingly in, coming down across our tail from starboard and above. O'Hare took position on our starboard wing, Skon on the port, bright blue in the flare of their exhausts, six guns jutting out of their wings. Canopy back, goggles up, yellow Mae West, khaki shirt, and helmet, Butch O'Hare sat aggressively forward, looking like the tough navy ace he was, his face sharply illuminated by his canopy light for one last brief instant.

The Japanese 752 Air Group reported losing three planes on the night of November 26, and sinking two carriers and one battleship. They also reported seeing more than three night fighters turn on their lights. This had to be the brief moment when our group, together for the only time that night, was illuminated, and it was at that point that, attracted by our lights, one of the Bettys tried to join up on us. The long black cigar shape came in on the starboard side of the group across the rear of O'Hare, and realizing its fatal mistake, began firing. "Butch, this is Phil. There's a Jap on your tail. Kernan, open fire." I began shooting at the Betty. The air was filled with streams of fire, and a long burst nearly emptied my ammunition can. The Betty, as the tracers arced toward him, continued firing and then abruptly disappeared into the dark to port. I thought I saw O'Hare reappear for a moment, and then he was gone. Something whitish gray appeared in the distance, his parachute or the splash of the plane going in. Skon slid away. I thought that the Jap had shot O'Hare and then disappeared, but I also realized with a sinking feeling that there was a chance I might have hit O'Hare as well in the exchange of fire.

Phillips took us down to drag the surface for a long half hour before we gave up and made our way back to the *Enterprise* at about 2100. Skon landed first without any trouble. But for us the evening was not over. We still had to make a landing on an unlighted carrier deck at night. If it had been done before, it was certainly not standard procedure, and Phillips, despite having a thousand hours as an instrument instructor, had never done it in practice. We homed on the white wake that marked the ship in the water, but there was no light anywhere on deck except the fluorescent wands of the landing signal officer standing on the end of the flight deck. We came in too high, and just as Phillips was about to cut the engine the landing signal officer waved us off. Full throttle, nearly stalling out, wheels, flaps, and hook down, we hung for an eternal moment above the deck, neither rising nor falling. I saw the huge, dark shape of the carrier's island structure just a few feet off our starboard wing, the parked planes on the deck just a few feet below, the men standing there looking up at us. We hung there, then picked up speed and flew away to go around again.

The *Enterprise* captain, Matt Gardner, must have known we would never make it with the cumbersome plane in the dark, so he turned on the shaded lights that marked out the flight deck for the crucial moment. They could only be seen from low and aft by a plane approaching for a landing, so they didn't reveal the ship very much for very long to a submarine or any Bettys still flying about. This time it worked. We dropped heavily on the deck. The corpsmen took Rand away, Phillips disappeared to talk to the admiral, and I made my way to the head just below the flight deck, where I stood and pissed for what seemed like five minutes. On and on it went, emptying all the accumulated fear and tension out with the water that had built up in the longest three hours of my life, before or since.

My first encounter with media arrogance came before I was out of the head. Eugene Burns, an Associated Press correspondent, came charging in and while I was still standing at the urinal trough asked, "What happened? Where were they? How many? Where is O'Hare? How many did you shoot down?" The tone was harshly aggressive, and I didn't feel like talking about it to anyone as abrasive and unpleasant as this guy. He bored right in, though, and began to try to construct the scandal he wanted. "How far away from O'Hare were you when he was hit? Were you shooting too?" And then, there it was: "Did you hit him?"

Really messy firefights don't sort themselves out in the head very clearly, either sooner or later, and heavy feelings of responsibility and guilt lurk around all combat deaths. Without doubt I had fired at the trailing Japanese plane that had tried to join up on us, and he had fired at everything in his range, including O'Hare and us, but had I, blasting away, hit the group commander as well? Had I been trigger-happy as a result of my disorientation and hearing O'Hare saying that he was about to begin shooting? Like the cigar-shaped Betty sliding out of the darkness to our rear, guilt slid across my mind. Letting me know that he was somehow an official who had a right to news and that anything of interest belonged to the public, Burns played on my doubts and shock to try to get me to blurt out some sudden, unconsidered remark that could be turned into sensational fare for his readers. If he had come at me with more sympathy I might have tried to tell him how mixed up it all was, but his bullying got my back up, and I walked off shouting, "Get the hell away from me." He went off muttering about reporting me to the officers, as if I had broken some kind of rule by not telling his newspaper everything, but he never came back. I suppose a public relations officer got hold of him, and in the end he wrote some embarrassingly wild stories, far more fiction than fact, for magazines like the *Saturday Evening Post,* describing O'Hare going down amid a blaze of gunfire while saving a grateful fleet, with bouquets to everyone involved, including me. The official navy version was not so garish, but it downplayed the fatal separation of the fighter planes and the torpedo plane, bringing them together much earlier than they had in fact joined up, and crediting the entire group, not Phillips alone, with two certain, and two possible, kills.

The intelligence officer gave me a cup of his famous coffee and debriefed me. Phillips, unsure of what had happened since he had been facing forward, away from the fight, went down to the sick bay to see Rand before he came to recap the flight with me and to get my view of what had happened. After he had put all the pieces together he accepted Rand's view. Rand, staring hard out of the tunnel window, had a good view of the exchange of fire and later described it with Yankee brevity: "Butch got lost and sought enlightenment by turning on recognition lights in front of a Japanese bomber. The Jap shot up Butch's can and Al Kernan shot the Jap."

Later I sat on the deck in a corner of the ready room for a long time talking to a few friends, Boone and Varner mostly, trying to sort the whole thing out. I tried to sleep, but air-conditioned cold—usually a luxury—made me feel that I was dead. Everyone else was comfortable, snoring away, so it was in my head, but it didn't go away. Shivering, I went over the fight again and again, trying to sort it out and only tangling it up more. I began to brood about bad luck, having had the orders to flight school that would have sent me back to the States rather than sitting here waiting to get killed, if not tonight then tomorrow, when we would be sure to go up again, having had so much success tonight.

Phillips was quite buoyed up by being credited with two enemy kills, unheard of for a torpedo pilot. O'Hare was recommended for another Congressional Medal of Honor, but in the end everyone on the flight received the Navy Cross, which surprised me since enlisted men usually got a lesser medal than the officers. Phillips became the group commander. But we still sat and waited the next two nights for another Black Panther flight, and once we got up to the deck and into the planes. But at the last minute the radar contact faded, and the flight was called off.

By the next night we were gone—Tarawa and Makin having been secured—on our way to attack the Marshall Islands, from which the Bettys had come, with the goal of knocking out the airfields and shipping in preparation for an invasion next month. Death still followed us, and on November 30 one of our planes loaded with depth charges crashed in the water alongside the ship while on antisubmarine patrol. While we watched the crew swimming in the water, the depth charges exploded.

The morning of the attack, December 4, 1943, was cool, the sun just rising as we sat on the hangar deck with the breeze blowing through the open curtains. We were to be the last off and were alone. I stood by the plane looking at the sun, wondering, as many going into battle must have wondered since time began, how I had gotten to that particular place when so many others who had more at stake were not there. Dark thoughts soon passed and fate was accepted in the excitement of taking off and taking the lead of the entire air group on the way to the target. From twenty thousand feet the whole atoll of Kwajalein spread out before us in an enormous boomerang of narrow, white-beached islands, with a big lagoon in the center, dark blue here, light there. The morning was beautiful, visibility unlimited. In the lagoon several Japanese ships were getting under way. Black antiaircraft bursts rocked the plane, and the fighter planes taking off from Roi-Namur far below seemed more interesting than ominous. A Japanese float plane going the other way flew by us, but no one recognized it until after it had passed, and there was no point in firing.

As dive-bombers attacked the ships and the fighters strafed the Japanese planes on the ground, we proceeded in a lordly way southward across the lagoon to the largest island, Kwajalein, at the southern tip, to glide-bomb—a shallower run than dive-bombing—the ground installations and the shipping in the anchorage. Phillips circled and watched, calling attention to targets, and as the last planes finished their runs and left, we went in alone to bomb a merchant ship. We pushed over from twenty thousand feet, and as we neared the bottom of our run through the thick antiaircraft fire, Phillips began firing his guns, which seemed rather odd. As we pulled up and I thought gratefully, "Now I can go to San Francisco," Phillips came on the intercom and admitted wryly that in the dive he had made the mistake of pressing the gun trigger on the front of the stick rather than the bomb release on the top of the stick. Too bad, I thought, but let's get the hell out of here and get me off to flight school. The thought never occurred to him, and around we went for another run, with everything in the area shooting at us. Our bombs seemed to hit the ship, but the painfully learned fact is that it is almost always impossible to tell for certain, even with photographs, and those who make bomb runs are understandably overly optimistic about results.

The return to Pearl Harbor was quiet, and I said goodbye to everyone and flew with Phillips and Sullivan for the last time to Pearl Harbor, from which I went to Ewa, the marine field where those going to flight training out of the fleet were assembled. O'Hare's memory was honored in time by the naming of the largest airport in the United States, O'Hare Field in Chicago, after him. Phillips was killed a few months later at Truk. As air group commander he had shifted from a torpedo plane to a fighter. No one saw what happened, and the plane was never found in the Truk lagoon, which had every kind of wreckage imaginable, but the reasoning was that while he was directing the attack a Japanese fighter came in on him from the rear.

TEN

Solo

One of the advantages the United States had over the Japanese was the ability to replace its losses, including its skilled manpower. At the beginning of the war the Japanese had trained a superior group of naval aviators, but they didn't have a replacement cadre. It was as if they thought the first group so good that they could never die. But the first group died with great bravery in one battle after another, and their places were then taken by recruits with only a few hours of training and no battle experience. The U.S. Navy, however, put an effective pilot-training program into place before the war and continued to produce a steady stream of replacements. By 1943 heavy casualties were expected, and the number of trainees was increased. Enlisted men from the fleet could apply, and this is how I got my chance to be a pilot and an officer at the beginning of 1944.

I went back by ship to San Diego, where I was given a train ticket to San Francisco and told to report to naval headquarters and be assigned to flight training. I stopped to see the Boones, who were, as always, most hospitable. The oldest son of the family, Bill, was an operator who had contacts with everyone, including Frank Sinatra, who was just then extremely popular. Bill took me to one of Sinatra's radio programs and introduced us. The great man was extremely pleasant and invited me to his house, to a party that never seemed to end. I never talked to Sinatra again, but the drinks were free and the girls rather remarkable. Someone asked me if I had any gas coupons, gas being rationed at that time. When I said, "No," he produced a big wad, all counterfeit or stolen, I suppose, but I took them gratefully and used them to drive around when I got leave. Bill Boone also knew people on the *Los Angeles Times* and arranged for pictures and interviews with me about the death of Butch O'Hare. I was cautious about the media after my brush with Eugene Burns, and it must have showed since the published article styled me "modest little Alvin Kernan." Bill sent a copy to his brother Dick and he, to my chagrin, later sent me a letter addressed to "Modest Little Alvin Kernan."

It was near Christmas when I got to San Francisco, and I expected to get some kind of leave, but since I had had thirty days' leave the previous March, I had used up my quota for that year and was ordered to report to flight training right away. Complaints about it being Christmas and about having missed out on leave in 1942 got me nowhere, but when I produced a fifth of good whiskey the Boones had given me the yeoman delayed my assignment until a later class, thus requiring me to take a thirty-day leave. I took up residence in the elegant Claremont Hotel on the ridge overlooking the bay in Oakland. In a few days I had just enough money left to buy a ticket to Saratoga.

It was bitterly cold in Wyoming, and, having fêted me only nine months earlier, the people had heard my sea stories and were rather unenthused to see me home again so soon. The comings and goings of servicemen, many of whom had been in combat, were getting commonplace. My old friends were all in the service by now, and the girls had all gotten married or had gone out to work in the California aircraft factories, and besides, after my spree in Oakland, I was flat broke. Frank Kernan, my stepfather, couldn't help. He had been elected justice of the peace, which meant that he could fine speeders and hunters and fishermen who were caught with too many deer or fish. He ran a small store in Saratoga, sold insurance, repaired electrical appliances, and kept a line of small gifts and greeting cards. I slept on a spare bed in the back of the store and drove around the county on icy roads with my illegal gas coupons looking for old friends and making dates with girls in Medicine Bow and Rawlins, all of whom, with great good sense, had different things in mind from me.

In the end I was glad to go back to California, realizing somehow that I had left Wyoming for good and that I would never go back to stay. Los Angeles was warm and lively for a few days, but by the time I got to San Luis Obispo in late January, the winter rains had set in and life got difficult. Flight prep school was designed mostly as a way of physically toughening up the V-5 cadets and was run by a bunch of old coaches from high schools and colleges who delighted in putting us—for our own good of course—through endless exercises, obstacle courses, endurance swims, long-distance runs, speed-agility tests, and so on. The marines among us, yellow from the Atabrine they had taken to prevent malaria, were tough, but most of us sailors were soft from sitting around too much and eating too many beans. Leaping over low walls, climbing ropes, and running cross-country came hard and painfully, but we were young and keen. Better here, it seemed, than back in the Pacific where the great drive across the center of the ocean toward Japan was rolling in high gear. The studies—aeronautics, meteorology, Morse code, navigation—seemed easy enough until I got cocky and failed a major navigational test—carelessly starting the original heading 180 degrees in the wrong direction—and had to attend remedial classes.

Mostly it rained, and we lined up outside our barracks at six in the morning, standing in the pouring rain, day after day. We worked, stood guard, ran to class, exercised, and ate, always damp and cold. Colds were endemic. Midway through the three-month course we were given a thirty-six-hour liberty, from noon on Saturday to midnight on Sunday. San Luis Obispo is about equidistant from Los Angeles and San Francisco, about two hundred miles either way. The entire coast was loaded with military camps, and there must have been a million soldiers, sailors, and marines in that area, many of them trying to get on the few buses and trains for the weekend. The bus depot where I went to catch a ride to Los Angeles looked like the hold of an immigrant ship, and I would never have gotten on the bus except for the help of a friend, a former marine sergeant named Joey Bishop. An Oklahoma Indian, he was short, dark, wiry, and a Guadalcanal veteran. He had helped me get through some of the more difficult parts of the training, like hand-to-hand combat and all-out wrestling, at which he excelled and I did not. He instantly saw that getting aboard the bus in the normal way, through the front door, was hopeless, and without hesitating, he went up the high side of the bus and into one of the open windows, holding out a hand to help me up and through. It was dark by the time we got to Los Angeles, and we immediately headed for the bars.

By noon the next day it was time to try to board another bus to take our dreadful hangovers back to San Luis Obispo. We got there by midnight, cold and exhausted, and then I stood watch from midnight to 0400, trying desperately to stay awake, while the rain never stopped dripping off the eaves. At the end of the three-month course, there was a ball for the graduating class. With travel and accommodations what they were, it all seemed pretty hopeless, but girls came from all over the country to go to dinner in the mess hall, dance in the local hotel and stay there with chaperones, and walk the next day on Pismo Beach, famous for its clams. No matter what the difficulties, the war was the most exciting show in town, worth any amount of inconvenience. I persuaded Betty Boone to come up for the occasion. Her mother came along, to Betty's chagrin, to make sure that she was safe, and paid for it by spending the dance night in her hotel listening to the drunken soldiery shout obscenities in the street below as they hurled bottles at the wall of the hotel. We three walked up and down Pismo Beach the next day, not knowing what to say, and in the afternoon the Boones departed, gratefully, for Los Angeles.

Flight training school, where we would actually get to fly an airplane, was the next step, and the next day we all went off to various desolate little flying fields in the northwest to learn to fly, first Piper Cubs, and then the yellow open-cockpit biplanes, N2Ss. I went into a school run by a Portland college, Lewis and Clark, out in the desert on the eastern border of Oregon, in a small town called Ontario, near the Snake River. We rode for days on a new kind of short boxcar that had been fitted up with shipboard-type bunks to transport troops, standing at the open doors like hoboes looking out at the countryside. Lewis and Clark, with few students during the war, was keeping alive by running this program and had transformed an old barn into a dormitory, mess hall, and classroom, next to a small macadamized flying field with one modest hangar and two short runways.

We were soon in the cabin of the little Piper Cubs, with the instructor sitting in back, taking off into the pale, sunny Oregon sky. After flying for years in the backseats of warplanes, the light plane with its washing-machine engine sounded a bit risky, but it moved around with agility and it was reassuringly safe, coming out of spins easily and gliding for miles without power. Turns, climbs, dives, spins, stalls, slips: we practiced for two hours a day, six days a week. Takeoffs and landings were the trickiest part, mostly because of strong crosswinds. To land in a crosswind you had to come in high on the leeward side of the runway and then slip down to the end of the runway, just a few feet above ground, pull level, and stall the plane out into a nice smooth landing. At first there was usually a heavy bump, and the plane would bounce back into the air and come down with another bang. Some of these heavy landings ruined propellers and too many washed you out, as did ground loops that came from getting caught by the crosswind or applying too much of the wrong brake while rolling down the field. You were supposed to solo after six to ten hours of instruction, and most of us did.

Flying may have been what we were interested in, but there was still daily physical training. There was a fiendish obstacle course and other devices that we learned soon to cheat by running with our heads turned watching the coach. When he looked away we dived through the lower rungs of contraptions we were supposed to climb and ran around walls we were supposed to jump over. He knew we were a bunch of slackers and put great store in the "step test" as a scientific way of demonstrating our lack of fitness. You stepped up on a knee-high bench and then stepped down, thirty times a minute for five minutes. Sounds easy, but it was very tiring. Our fitness was determined by the speed with which the pulse returned to normal. I had low blood pressure to begin with, so my heart rate didn't have far to go to get back to normal, and on the chart I always registered as extremely fit. Since the coach had me down as a goof-off and a miserable athlete, my scores infuriated him, but he seems never to have thought of determining whether we all began with the same pulse rate. His faith in the uniformity of nature was as absolute as it was unwarranted.

The town of Ontario was a pleasant little place to which we could go frequently, there being almost no discipline in the barracks. Liquor was rationed and sold only in state stores, but you could keep your weekly bottle in a locker club, and if you wanted a drink you would give the bartender a key and he would solemnly open a wooden locker where your whiskey was stored. For only a modest service charge he would pour out a shot, return the bottle to the locker, give you back the key, and provide ice and whatever else was needed.

As soon as we learned to fly the Cubs we were clamoring to get into the Yellow Perils, and we did so after a month. This was different: more power, an open cockpit, more response on the controls. After a few hours of instruction in these biplanes we began to fly them solo for two hours each day, each plane being sent out to a separate sector somewhere above the Oregon desert, keeping track of your position by watching the Snake River, practicing one maneuver after another. On our own with airplanes, we became adventurous, and there were games like flying under bridges—recklessly dangerous considering how inexperienced we were as pilots. The worst, and therefore the most delightful, stunt was to find a stretch of straight highway without telephone poles and fly along it with the wheels just off the ground. The trick here was to catch a car coming from the opposite direction and fly straight at him and then come back on the stick and jump over the terrified driver. The natives came to loathe us, quite justly, and called in regularly with the plane number to report us. We were real menaces to the life and limbs of others as well as ourselves, and only in wartime would the countryside have put up with us.

Unexpectedly my medal for the night-fighter battle came through. Twenty-five or thirty cadets lined up to hear the station commander read the citation and pin the Navy Cross on me. I wore the medal—one of the few times in my life I ever had a chance to wear it—while we all went into the mess hall and ate the cinnamon buns for which the cook was famous. Then I put it in its box to keep and pass on to my children. It all seemed askew, sitting there munching warm buns in homey surroundings and remembering the wild night for which the medal was awarded. The Navy Cross carried with it a monthly payment of three dollars, which in time I duly got and drew for the remainder of my time in the navy. The circumstances of my award, though strange, were nowhere near as odd as those of Hazen Rand, the radar officer in the Black Panther TBF. He was carried off to sick bay with a Japanese bullet in his foot, nothing serious it was thought, but the wound took years to heal. He also caught some kind of crud in the hospital that was only cured after he got home when he was painted blue all over with fungicide and immersed to the waist in a barrel of gasoline. It took many years for his Navy Cross to catch up with him, and when they decorated him in a stateside hospital they had to borrow one. The medal finally arrived, years later, and the Navy Department sent him two.

The heavy casualties the navy had prepared for in the Pacific had not materialized, and by now there were far too many pilots in training. One way of delaying the problem of what to do with them was to give them leave, and we were, at the end of our three months in Ontario, sent off for fifteen days. I thought that with my new officer's uniform, though without any stripes, I would cut quite a swath in Saratoga. But the town was dead, with all the men my age gone by now, and I hung around for a few days without much to do and then headed out to Los Angeles to see the Boones. Then I went up to Santa Rosa, where the old squadron, Torpedo 6, was re-forming before going to sea again.

The other thing the navy could do to relieve the glut of pilots in training was to extend the already long time of pilots' training by adding more steps along the way. Having been to flight prep and flight training, I now went to preflight school at Saint Mary's College, in Walnut Creek, California, just east of Oakland, where there were no airplanes and we did no flying. We studied more navigation, did endless physical training, and spent hours in the pool. I learned to swim four different strokes and to stay afloat in the pool for six hours with my clothes on, without getting any closer to flying. Like many naval stations by the summer of '44, Saint Mary's fielded numerous athletic teams, largely made up of professional athletes who had enlisted or been drafted—the navy was drafting men by now—and were kept around simply to play various games and add luster to the navy. The football team at Saint Mary's was a rough bunch who had trouble finding someone to practice against. The solution was close at hand. Cadets were issued football uniforms and sent out to provide the team with raw meat as a part of our PT, physical training. We never got the ball; we only lined up for them to block and to run over. But this group of old sailors wasn't having any of it. The coaches exhorted us to stand up like men and threatened us with extra drill and diminished liberty, but each time the center gave the ball to the quarterback on the professional team, we all instantly dropped where we were and covered up our heads with our arms. The backs got some pleasure, I suppose, out of running over us, but we kept our teeth intact and avoided broken bones.

About this time the navy openly admitted for the first time that they had too many pilots in training and that we could expect at the least about another year of training, the length of the full program at the time we began, before we would get our wings. To many it seemed fine. Some risk in training accidents, but better than going out to the fleet again when the war was getting closer to the Japanese homeland. To the kids who joined pilot training direct from civilian life, there really wasn't much alternative since they would be sent to boot camp as apprentice seamen, starting at the bottom of the ladder. For many of us who came from the fleet, however, the extended training was the last straw. V-5 was a dog's life, no freedom at all, constant running here and there being shouted at by a bunch of amateur officers who had never been to sea, studying the same subjects over and over. I decided that I would rather take my chances, get my rating of first-class ordnanceman back, and live a more exciting life. So I resigned from V-5 and got a little paper thanking me for my patriotism and a ticket to Chicago and the Great Lakes naval training station, where all the ex-cadets went to be reassigned.

We were put in a huge wooden hangar filled with double-decker bunks. As our old uniforms were sent to us from home, we began to look like real sailors again, sitting around day after day with nothing to do. Even card playing was out since we had no money, our pay records being in an administrative shuffle somewhere.

There was one diversion—going to parties at night. The people of that area were almost hysterical with hospitality. A serviceman couldn't walk down the street without someone trying to get him to come home for a meal, join in a family party, stay the night. Milwaukee was famous for this kind of generosity, and whenever you felt like a strenuous party you took the Skokie Valley Express, a terrifying train of old trolley cars that rattled seventy miles an hour from Chicago up to Milwaukee. As you came out of the train people were waiting on the platform to round up servicemen for one kind of a party or another. Since then, as now, there was entertainment and there was entertainment, the trick was to spot and join a group of patriots represented by pretty girls that looked like it made drinking and dancing part of the fun, rather than going to a church service or looking at family pictures. If your constitution was robust you would go with one of the many Polish groups: strong young men, faces red with effort and hernias threatening to explode, holding beer kegs overhead until everyone filled their mugs. Endless polkas going faster and faster. I can still hear the stomping of the "Beer Barrel Polka"—"Roll out the barrel, we'll have a barrel of fun"—louder and louder, faster and faster. The girls, all of whom had reverted to their native Polish costumes, were beautiful and devoted to nothing but dancing, faster and faster, no pause for anything else. Finally, exhausted and beery, you were taken back to the Skokie Valley Express in the early hours of the morning to rattle—every rattle inside the head as well as in the wheels—back to Chicago. After having your morale lifted in an aerie of Polish Falcons, you were glad to sit around and breathe quietly for a day or two.

There were again few restrictions on our movements, and we ought to have enjoyed liberty in a wonderful liberty town, but we were always broke. I finally moved into Chicago—no permission needed since there were no roll calls—took a hotel room, and got a daytime job working in the package section of the post office, unloading the mail. It was bitterly cold in the shed and the heavy mailbags stuffed with packages were hard on the hands, but we were paid at the end of each day. After a time I moved to a better-paying hourly job in a small defense plant in an old factory, loading with one other sailor four-hundred-pound iron bars on a tottering dolly and pushing it onto a rickety elevator, up to another floor, where the bars were lifted off the dolly to another pile. I never knew what happened to them or what the plant made—possibly nothing at all—but at five each day the boss would give us cash for whatever hours we had worked. My hotel demanded payment daily, and after I had bought a meal and paid the daily rent there was nothing left over, and so the next day I would go to the factory again and wrestle with iron bars until it was time to eat and fall into bed exhausted. I stuck with this routine for about a week, calling in each day to be sure that no orders had come for me to report to duty someplace. Then the pointlessness of it began to seep in. I went back to the training station and wangled a week's leave. I decided to let chance decide where to spend the leave, went to the Greyhound bus depot, and asked how far twelve dollars and something, my accumulated savings from work in the defense factory, would take me "riding the Dawg."

It would, it turned out, take me quite a distance: to Bemidji, Minnesota, one of the record cold spots in the country, right up near the Canadian border. I wired Ruth Emery, collect, and she agreed to meet me in Minneapolis. Having worked in Valley City for the last year she was about to set out for a new job teaching in Salem, Oregon. I was taking advantage of her: she paid all the bills, for she cared more for me by a lot than I for her. We were both too tense. She wanted an engagement, even knowing that I was surely one of the last candidates in the world for marriage, by either circumstance or inclination. Pleading the dangers of the war I reluctantly put her on the bus for Salem and took another bus north.

The Lord did provide, for I soon got to talking to another sailor, Curt, going home on leave. He was a reader, as I was, and we talked happily of books. I was reading John Dos Passos's trilogy *USA* at the time. Curt had had a year of college and praised Thomas Wolfe, Hemingway, Fitzgerald, and other American authors. Asked where I was going, I replied that I had a ticket to Bemidji and hoped to find a place to stay when I got there. He at once invited me to stay at his house, and I did for a couple of days, talking and going fishing for pickerel with him in the nearby lake. His leave was short, and he was off soon. After the war I tried to call Curt to see if he had made it. He had not, but died in an unusual way. Stabbed, his mother said, by a lunatic stranger who came up to him on a Chicago street and put a knife in his heart. Mistaken identity or mindless fury, no one knew.

Two girls who worked for the local dentist arranged for me to stay with the family of one of them, where I was fed and treated like a hero. During the day I would hang around the dental office—the dentist never seemed to be there—sitting in the chair and flirting with the girls. They would clean my teeth from time to time, treat my gums, and provide other dental services. An odd kind of an interlude, but I remember it as a luxuriance associated closely with the mouth and the teeth. In a day or so it was time to go back to Chicago, and the local American Legion provided a rail ticket.

For many, one of the vivid memories of World War II must be sitting up, desperately tired, trying to find some way to sleep in a rattling railroad day coach, with constant movement up and down the aisle, drafts, lights, smells of apples and orange peels. Shifting this way and that, trying to find some way of stretching the legs. After one of those nights, I was back in Chicago, stiff, exhausted, hoping to God there would at last be orders sending me to some kind of regular duty. There were. I had hoped that after two tours of overseas duty I would get to stay stateside for a while. But the orders were for Torpedo Squadron 40, a squadron that had been land-based on Guadalcanal in late 1943 to attack the Japanese bases in the Solomons and Rabaul. Now they had been joined with a fighter squadron to form a small air group to go on an escort carrier.

I was soon off to Los Alamitos, California, a navy field just to the northeast of Long Beach, where VT-40 was in training. Another long train ride back to the California sunshine, but when I got to Los Alamitos in early November, the squadron had transferred to Livermore, about twenty miles to the east of San Francisco Bay. I was given a ticket and sent on my way once more, but I couldn't pass up a chance to see the Boones again, and their hospitality was so warm that I decided to spend a full day sitting around with them. When I did arrive at Livermore I assumed that no one would note the missing day, but the personnel officer did. I had no acceptable explanation, so all I could say was that I had come along as fast as I could, missed trains, and some other mumblings, all as indistinct as possible. This seemed, to my surprise, to challenge him. He was a by-the-book character, and he used to pop up from time to time, hoping to catch me off guard, I think, and ask me why I had been a day late in reporting.

Livermore in November and December was foggy and cold, with no heat in the barracks. We sat around in light clothing, shivering, waiting for the fog to clear so that training flights could go up, but most days we were grounded. Although I was an aerial gunner, there was no crew that needed me. I was not sorry: in all that fog there were many accidents, and I happily worked in the ordnance ground crew. I found no one in the squadron I had known before, but made one of the few close friends I made in the navy. Jim Loughridge, from near Buffalo, was a dapper young man, a lot more culturally sophisticated than I was, and I learned a great deal from him about how to live well in even unpromising circumstances. He shared my growing interest in books, and we sat in bars talking about books like Arthur Koestler's *Darkness at Noon* and James Joyce's *Ulysses*. We went into San Francisco to the opera, or at least the operetta, *Student Prince;* we searched out good restaurants, and on New Year's Eve, for the first time in my life, I drank champagne—wartime champagne, but festive nonetheless. Ruth came down from Salem—this time I paid—but again it was an awkward meeting, lying stiffly in bed side by side and not talking. She laughed at my newfound sophistication, which annoyed me and made me think she was content to go on being a country girl while I had larger aspirations. After a short stay she went back to Oregon, depressed.

Loughridge came down with some mysterious disease and was sent off to a hospital. He had been flying with the commanding officer, Lieutenant Campbell, and I now took over his turret for a few flights. Campbell was as dour as his name, and we didn't get along very well, so we soon parted. But at least the personnel officer stopped asking me about the missing day.

Cigarettes were now in short supply everywhere, and Ceil Boone, who smoked like a chimney, as they used to say, was suffering from nicotine privation. She asked me to send cigarettes, any cigarettes I could find, and I did. We were rationed at the ship's store, and since I smoked heavily myself, I had used up what I could buy that way. There were, however, numerous cigarette machines about the base, and armed with lots of change I went around getting packages of some of the strangest brand names I ever saw and mailing off care packages to Mrs. Boone. Knowing what we know now about smoking, it seems almost criminal that the services supported smoking the way they did with cheap cigarettes. But no one knew at the time the connection with various diseases, and smoking was one of the few pleasures that could be indulged while caught in the endless waiting that war requires. So we all puffed away, and paid the price, as I did with a heart attack, many years later.

I began flying again with Bob Dyer, one of the new ensigns who made up most of the squadron, who was known as "Irish," from Illinois, and with his radioman, Oscar Mullins, a Georgia boy with a dish face, inevitably called "Moon" after the old comic-strip character Moon Mullins. In early February orders came to move the planes and the crews to the Alameda naval air station, adjacent to where the Bay Bridge comes into Oakland. For a few days we were in barracks there, given liberty in San Francisco every night. We longed to stay at the Mark Hopkins Hotel, the setting of a wildly popular novel, *Shore Leave,* by Frederic Wakeman, telling the story of a group of pilots returning from the Pacific after a long cruise who took rooms in the Mark, got fabulously drunk, exchanged brilliant wit, and reeled from one beautiful girl to another. The actuality, however, was going down to the USO and drinking free coffee, hoping to get a chance to dance with one of the few weary girls who were grimly doing their part in the war effort by being friendly with the servicemen. They were nice girls, I thought, but inevitably they ended up having to wrestle with one of the most unwashed of the soldiers and sailors, crying out for help only when they seemed to be in actual danger, as they often were. When the shore patrol hauled off the culprits, usually after banging them on the head with a club for a bit, the girls would look stricken, feeling somehow responsible for the lust they had aroused, however innocently. I had always assumed, like most men, that men had it a lot harder in this life than women, but I learned in that USO how hard it is for young women, and some not so young, to deal with the sex they cannot escape.

Sailors everywhere and at all times know that no matter how hard sea duty, there is always relief in going aboard ship and leaving land behind. So it was again on February 8, 1945, when we picked up our gear and went aboard the USS *Suwanee* (CVE-27), lying at the Alameda dock. Converted from a tanker, she was an awkward, slow, unattractive old waddler with very cramped crew's quarters. But she had been on more invasions than any other navy ship, from North Africa to the Philippines, where her flight deck had been blown off the day the Japanese fleet broke into Leyte Gulf to take the support ships under fire. Go to the carrier museum on board the *Yorktown* in Charleston Harbor and you will find that two escort carriers, the *Suwanee* and the *Liscombe Bay*, suffered more casualties than any other aircraft carrier in the war.

The planes were hoisted aboard, and we were ready to sail, but two of the old hands from Torpedo 40 were still missing as the gangways began to come up. Then a broken-down car came roaring down to the dock, pulling right up to the edge at high speed and screeching to a stop. Both sailors jumped out, running for the last gangway, and then one turned back, opened the driver's door, released the brake, and gave the car a push off the end of the dock into San Francisco Bay. The crew stood on the deck cheering wildly as Cletis Powell leaped across several feet of water to land in the well deck and ask the officer-of-the-deck for permission to come aboard. It was a gallant gesture, but Powell should have missed the ship.

Leaving San Francisco Bay, sailing under the reddish Golden Gate Bridge, picking up the long Pacific swells, and looking back on the white cities on the hills was one of the great experiences of the Pacific war. It was powerful not only in retrospect, as so many events are after the future is known, but at the moment it took place. We were at quarters in undress blue uniforms, lining the flight deck as we went under the bridge, and the ship's horn sounded a salute to the country left behind and got in return blasts from all the other ships in the harbor. It was valedictory, a moving, powerful sensory image of a country united in war and determined to win it. Every man must have wondered whether he would ever come back again—I know I did—and wondered too how many of those standing with him would return. This was my third combat tour, and I knew what would happen. My eyes moved from one face to another of men who are as alive to me now as they were then, but whose bones are washing around the bottom of the sea, tangled in the wreckage of their planes between Okinawa and Taiwan, near islands with such romantic names as Ishigaki, Miyako, and Kerama-retto.

ELEVEN

War's End

By February 16 we were at Pearl Harbor. We crossed the International Date Line on February 28 and the equator on March 2. The day before I got a ducking when we crashed on a catapult launch. The catapult was a long rail running about fifty feet to the forward edge of the flight deck, with a trolley that ran inside the rail. A plane would be positioned at the rear of the catapult rail, and the trolley was attached to its wheels by two cables leading up to hooks on the inside wheel struts. At the rear the plane would be anchored by a hook attached to the deck by means of a tension ring just strong enough to hold the plane in place when it was turned up to full power. As the plane maneuvered into position, the cables were attached to the struts, and the anchor was hooked up. Then the plane turned up to full power, and after straining at the leash for several seconds, the catapult trolley was fired forward by an explosive charge. The combined power of the engine and the trolley broke the retaining ring at the tail, and the plane jumped forward, down the deck, to be airborne at the edge.

Usually it all went like clockwork, but on March 1, as we sat on the catapult braced for takeoff, when the engine came to full power a defective retaining ring snapped. We began to lumber forward without enough speed to get airborne and toppled over the port side of the ship, down through the catwalk, shearing off metal as we went. Into the water we plunged, went under, and then bobbed up, nose down with the heavy engine. The ship went tearing by high above us. All I saw was Cletis Powell leaning out a porthole in the parachute loft where I had just lost seventy-five dollars to him at blackjack, on credit, yelling, "Al, you don't have to pay. Get out, get out, for God's sake."

No one in the plane was hurt, only disoriented. I made my way out the side of the turret onto the port wing; Mullins came out his tunnel door and got up onto the starboard wing. From opposite sides we opened the life raft stowage compartment, located just forward of the turret, and began pulling. Mullins was smaller and less determined than I, and I nearly pulled him through the stowage tunnel before he let go. I pulled the inflation toggle and the raft filled up satisfactorily, with a big hiss. We stepped in and paddled off with the aluminum oar provided. From the deck of the carrier it had seemed like a light sea, but in the yellow rubber raft we rose and fell ten or fifteen feet. We bobbed over to the plane guard, the destroyer that followed the carrier during landings and takeoffs for just such events, and pulled alongside. It loomed above us, letting lines down from the high bow, leaping up and slamming down in the swell. We swept into the side, the raft overturned and drifted away, and each of us grabbed a line to climb up to the deck. I banged against the side of the ship and was dazed and on the verge of drowning, with a lot of water inside me, until I let loose and drifted back amidships where the deck was much lower and more stable. I came over the side and was soon in a bunk with one of the small bottles of medical whiskey saved for such occasions. Next day the destroyer came alongside the carrier, fired a line over, and delivered us back aboard in a bosun's chair. We were flying again by that afternoon.

The ship had begun to heat up in the living quarters, which, on the *Suwanee*, were grim unpainted crammed cubicles. Bunks were in racks as high as five or six, the lights were always on, lockers were small, the heads were far away, so that going for a shower—always salt water—or to relieve yourself was a long walk, half-naked, through several eating and living compartments. It sounds like nothing now, but it built up pressure day after day, which increased as the temperature went up and we began suffering from heat rashes and raw places where a belt or a trouser leg chafed. It got worse when, on March 4, we anchored in Tulagi Harbor, just across Iron Bottom Bay from Guadalcanal, and there was no longer fresh air coming down the vents to cool the lower decks. The heat rose and the bugs began to make their way from land to feed on what the sea had brought them. We slept in our skivvies—the navy knew no pajamas—and would rise in the morning glad to get out of a "sack" that was damp with perspiration.

After a day or two we went ashore to Henderson Field on Guadal-canal, where a year and a half earlier the Japanese drive south was finally stopped. There had been a tremendous buildup of American forces on Guadalcanal since that time, but now the fighting had shifted away from the southwest Pacific and the island was nearly deserted. We could walk about looking at the muddy jungle swamps and sluggish rivers where so many desperate battles had taken place a short time ago. Elsewhere the Philippines had been retaken; Iwo Jima had recently been stormed by the marines; and the air force, with its B-29s, and the big navy carriers were at work on the mainland of Japan. As the war moved on, the troops had simply moved out of Guadalcanal, leaving, in that careless way of rich Americans, their buildings and a lot of machinery behind them. A library filled several Quonset huts, the books damp and smelling of mold in the rainy climate, and there was only one rule: "If you check a book out, you can't return it." The U.S. Navy Seabees—construction battalions—had left a big ice-making machine running for as long as the fuel in the tank for the engine driving the compressor held out. Beer was plentiful, huge stacks of cardboard cartons of it, with a single guard walking around. We were in a sailors' paradise for a few days—endless beer cooled to low temperatures in big Lister bags filled with ice.

The pilots had gone off on their own parties, and no one bothered us very much, so we lay naked, except for our white hats, in our bunks in one of the numerous empty Quonset huts on the edge of the airfield and drank beer and more beer and still more beer. Something odd began to happen as we drank more and more. It began with just smashing a few bottles on the plywood floor of the Quonset hut as we emptied them. Then, as the floor began to be covered with broken glass, the rule was that anyone wanting to go to the head or get another bottle of beer had to walk barefoot through the ever deepening layer of glass. At first it was possible to work your way around the biggest and sharpest shards of brown glass, but as more and more glass accumulated, the trip became more and more difficult and painful. But this problem was countered by rising drunkenness and its attendant indifference to reality, urged on by the need to piss more often and the desire to drink even more beer.

As each sailor rose from his bunk to try to make the door, cheers and groans accompanied him on his trip. If he winced or turned back he was hooted, if he cut himself and jumped in pain he was laughed at, if he strode bravely through the mess into the dark where the beer was—outside the door and the range of the single bulb burning in the center of the hut—he was cheered and awarded imaginary commendations. Basic anthropology: warriors' drinking and endurance rituals in the longhouse before battle.

In time the game wore itself out as people passed out or simply dropped off to sleep. But it started up again the next day, and anyone visiting the Quonset hut where the aircrew of VT-40 was quartered would have thought he had wandered into some madhouse filled with naked men with badly cut feet and blood all over a litter of broken glass. Then we were all back at sea, with painfully sore feet for a time. We left Tulagi, without nostalgia, on March 14, going north to that remarkable fleet anchorage, Ulithi Atoll, providing antisubmarine patrol for a convoy carrying a Marine Division for the landings on Okinawa on April 1. On the way north a destroyer pulled alongside with mail and transferred my friend Jimmy Loughridge, completely cured of whatever crud had felled him at Livermore, back aboard. Better for him if the crud had kept him in the hospital a bit longer, but no one knows beforehand the turns of fate.

Ulithi is a huge atoll out in the Pacific Ocean, halfway between the Philippines and Guam. The islands that made up the atoll are narrow coral-and-sand strips, only a few yards wide in places, running in a huge circle around an old sunken volcano, with deep blue water in the center. Here the navy had constructed a base for the final attack on Japan, and as we came into the atoll on our little gray escort carrier, the by-now almost unbelievable striking force of the Pacific Fleet was stretched out in front of us. Rows of new battleships, heavy and light cruisers, swarms of destroyers, and the new carrier battle force. The remaining two old carriers were there—the *Enterprise* and the *Saratoga*—and all the old names were there on new ships—*Lexington, Hornet, Yorktown, Wasp*—as well as new old ones like *Essex, Randolph, Franklin, Intrepid,* and on and on. It was the most powerful navy ever assembled and a heart-stirring sight to someone who had seen the burned-out battleship row at Pearl Harbor and had watched the *Enterprise,* the last operating carrier in the fleet, disappear over the horizon at Santa Cruz as the *Hornet* was sinking: "Proceed without *Hornet*."

Among a forest of repair facilities, an airfield, docks (including a huge floating drydock capable of taking any capital ship in the fleet), hospitals, storehouses, and so on, the navy's wisdom had decreed a recreation area for the sailors of the Pacific Fleet. Mog Mog—such was its memorable name—was a tiny islet with a small sand hill at one end and a mangrove swamp at the other. As those fortunate enough to get four hours of liberty, myself among them, came ashore onto the dock, a trail led inland to a

fork with a sign that read, "OFFICERS LEFT. ENLISTED PERSONNEL RIGHT."
The officers filed off up the sand hill to a club where beer and whiskey
were available in small amounts. It was crude but pleasant, I heard from
Irish Dyer, with even a beach and swimming.

To the right was a gate in a barbed-wire fence where the shore patrol
checked your liberty card and nodded at a chief standing by a huge pile
of cases of beer, who then handed you two cans of warm brew. Shiny aluminum cans in hand, you went up over a little rise and saw the swamp,
where by now all the foliage had been stripped and most of the trees and
bushes pulled down and stamped into a greasy mash of mud covered
with sailors in blue dungarees talking and drinking their two cans of beer.
Here and there a pipe had been driven into the soaked ground and a fun-
nel inserted into the end to make a crude urinal. These were in constant
use. Fights broke out now and again between crews of different ships,
and there were even a few drunks who had managed to buy nondrink-
ers' rations. Mostly, however, even hardened sailors, wild for liberty and
drink, blanched at the sight of Mog Mog, and there was—an unheard of
thing—a long line of men back at the landings waiting to return to their
ships. But having accepted liberty, like mankind getting freedom from
God, they could not return it until the appointed hour, when their launch
arrived to carry them away from this stygian lake.

Within a week we were at sea again, flying antisubmarine patrols for
transports on the way to Okinawa. On March 31 the other carriers of this
type, also named after small rural rivers in America—Sangamon, Santee,
and Chenango—joined up with the Suwanee to form a division to provide
close support to the soldiers and marines landing on Okinawa. On Easter
Sunday, April 1, the invasion began, and we started flying two and three
short strikes a day from about fifty miles offshore to the island, where we
circled until the control on the ground at the front called us in to hit a
particular target.

The landings were unopposed, the Japanese choosing not to sacrifice troops on the beaches. But the island was honeycombed with elaborate underground bunkers and stone tombs dug into the hills, where the Japanese had holed up and stored supplies. Most often our mission was to fly low up a small valley, come as close as possible to the mouth of a tomb, and then either sling a five-hundred-pound bomb into it or hit it with one or more of the eight five-inch rockets we carried under our wings. Sounds straightforward, but from the air it was nearly impossible, despite smoke signals on the ground, to make out the exact cave we were supposed to go after. And once it was located it was difficult to roar up a steep valley at 200 miles an hour, going close enough to hit the cave but leaving time to pull up and go over the ridge behind. We all worked hard at it and improved with time, but it was always a close thing and sometimes rockets were fired into our own lines when they were too close to the tombs' entrances.

A high cost began to be exacted at once, in the air as well as on the ground. The air group commander, Lieutenant Commander Sampson, was incredibly keen, pressing his attacks hard in his Hellcat to show others the way. He pressed so hard that he was dead in the first week. At the time he seemed to me to be old and grave, but looking back at photos, I see now that he was young, only in his late twenties I would guess, and I am reminded how much the war was the business of young men.

We stayed only a few days at Okinawa until we were sent south on April 8 to take over from a British fleet that had been keeping airfields on the Sakishima Islands, just northeast of Taiwan, unusable. The Japanese were flying whatever planes they had in China to dirt landing fields on two islands in this group—Ishigaki and Miyako—and then loading them with explosives and sending them north as suicide planes, kamikazes, against the invasion fleet and the big carriers. Our job was to continue keeping the fields so full of holes that landings and takeoffs were impossible, work which would go on for months, day after day.

April 13: Roosevelt died. The news was announced over the loudspeaker and brought everyone up short. It is hard to convey the way Roosevelt dominated our world, how he was the only leader we really remembered. He had presided over the terrible later years of the Depression when most of us aboard were growing up, and we remembered him for his "fireside chats" and his reassuring messages about the economy, even as things got worse and worse. He had taken us into the war, wanted it really, but most of us had also considered war against both Japan and Germany inevitable. It was simply in the cards in the late thirties. I had voted, by absentee ballot, for the first time the year before, and just to be different had cast my ballot for Wendell Wilkie rather than Roosevelt, but I had no real reasons for doing so, and now, like everyone else, I was troubled about who would make the decisions. About Truman we knew nothing, but we had no confidence in him for the days ahead, which looked depressingly bleak. We all assumed that there would be landings in Japan by the end of the year, and we feared them as nothing else in the war. After the war I heard a historian say that he had never met a veteran scheduled for the invasion who did not think there was a bullet in Japan that would end directly between his eyes. And he was right.

In the meantime the war went on. The landing signal officer brought a seagull on board, noting that he was "smooth on the controls." We were hurled roughly off the catapults, twice a day, early morning and early afternoon, and then once the next day, at midmorning. It became routine, but the early flights had a particular problem. Reveille was at four, breakfast was almost always beans, and we were launched before five in the dark. There was no time to shit, and as the altitude increased, the gas of the beans expanded and created terrible cramps. I refused to endure it, a veteran grown crusty in my ways at twenty-one, and drove Mullins up into the turret while I squatted on the floor of the tunnel and relieved myself on a piece of red rayon torn from a gunnery target sleeve. The plane had relief tubes that made it possible to urinate in flight, but the only way to be rid of my load was to tie a knot in the red rag, open one of the ventilators at the rear of the tunnel, fling it out, and idly watch out of one of the side ports as this bright "blivvie" made its way down through the second division flying below and to the rear. There was some protest about red rags plummeting down through the formation every other day, but no one ever got hit, and our crew stayed silent.

We lived in a narrow place and a removed time in which we bombed them and they shot at us. In which we put holes in their runways and they, with fiendish speed, filled them up again, and we came back and put more holes in the runways. We made our way back to the ships in a golden-green haze, with rainstorms and bright shafts of sunlight in a dozen different places around the horizon. The scene had a magical quality, intensified by the big lift that came from having survived another run. We feared the islands we bombed, and with good reason. The intelligence officer told us to avoid the swamps if we were shot down, so filled were they with leeches that you could die from loss of blood. We made our way down to the islands, dived on the rough airfields in the valleys below, dropped our bombs—usually a string of hundred-pounders—and fired our rockets. The antiaircraft fire was intense, and since our job was to bomb the runways we never attacked the guns directly. The Japanese learned in time that we never shot at them, so firing at us became an early form of Nintendo. At the bottom of our runs, when we were below the ridge lines, the guns were actually firing down at us, and I could fire furiously back at them.

Inevitably, there were casualties: April 25, Collura, Powell, to whom I still owed my blackjack losses, and Stewart were hit in a dive and went in and exploded; April 27, Campbell, the commanding officer, Jimmy Loughridge, my close friend, and Zahn were hit and disintegrated in the air. Death was unremarkable, but still it was difficult to accept that someone you knew well and had played cards with in a normal way only a few hours earlier was now gone forever, not a part of the same world, or any world for that matter, any longer. I wrote a childish, sentimental letter to Jimmy's widowed mother in Jamestown, New York, trying to say that he had lived and died well, but making a terrible mess of it. Sitting at a table in the mess compartment I heard that sharp, flat noise that could only be a bomb. I rushed up the ladders to the flight deck, and there was one of our planes, blackened and smoldering, with three bodies alongside.

Our bomb racks were tricky, and sometimes they would not release all the bombs but delay on one or two until you pulled out of the dive and the bomb-bay doors closed. Then the increased gravity would pull an unreleased bomb out of the rack onto the doors. When this happened the arming wire would pull out of the bomb fuse, and its propeller would turn freely in the bomb-bay draft until the bomb was armed. We knew about the problem, and radiomen were under strict orders after a run to look through the glass inset between the tunnel and the bomb bay to make sure that all the bombs were out of there. If they were not, the bomb bay was to be instantly opened with an emergency release in the tunnel and any remaining bombs shaken out by radical maneuvers. But the bomb bay was dark and difficult to see into when closed, and on this day the radioman had missed an armed hundred-pounder lying on the doors because a hydraulic line had been hit by antiaircraft fire and the fluid had obscured the glass window to the bomb bay. When the plane landed, caught the arresting wire, and came to an abrupt stop, the bomb slid forward until it hit the batteries just beneath the pilot, Slingerland, blowing him to kingdom come, and filling the gunner, Joyce, with so many small holes that the serum they poured into him ran right out again. He died that night. The radioman, Dick Morrow, was in a bad way but lived to become a fashionable dance band leader in the Detroit area.

Death was on my mind, for obvious reasons, those days flying to and from Ishigaki staring at "Hard Homo" in yellow letters on a dark green background of armor plate. I had read recently in the overseas edition of *Time,* a great favorite in the fleet, that there were "no atheists in foxholes," but it hadn't worked that way for me. I concluded that war's cruelty and randomness, its indifference to human life, and the speed and ease with which it erases existence are not aberrations but speeded-up versions of how it always is. The evidence is there, I went on to reason, to anyone who will look and see the plain facts his senses, including common sense, offer him—and what else is there to trust, fallible though they may be?— that men and women, like everything else in the world, are, in the poet's words, begotten, born, and die. A young man's raw desire to live made me avoid worrying about the bleakness of total extinction, but we all knew it; it was in our faces, it was the basis of our shared attitude toward one another and life.

There was a Jesuit chaplain aboard who was willing to argue about such questions, and I took advantage of his youthful good nature to play the village atheist. With a swaggering materialism I denounced Catholicism and all religion to the poor red-faced young Irish priest, who could not imagine that a young man brought up in the arms of holy mother the church, once an altar boy, could conceive of a world without a God or any purpose in life other than what we could give it. After a time I ceased tormenting the priest and concentrated on playing bridge, keeping a game going with the same players for weeks at a time, interrupting our playing on the coolness of the well deck only when someone had to fly, and picking up the hands as we had left them when the players returned. A Boston Irishman named Tom McCue, a former worker in a shipyard, was my partner, and we each developed a good sense of how the other bid and played. The waves splashed near us as we played, sitting on top of a big coil of manila rope, but anxious to perfect our skill we played with all the precise rules and formality of some fashionable bridge club in a tournament.

Although we kept the runways on Miyako and Ishigaki torn up, some Japanese planes got through to crash into the fleet. We were all terrorized by the kamikazes, for it is difficult to avoid someone trying to fly into you. The Japanese had always had a feel for the suicidal charge, and when the *Hornet* sank in 1942, two planes had crashed into her and exploded, one only a short distance from where I was sitting. But at the end of the war the "Divine Winds" had become the only effective Japanese weapon, and day after day the young pilots drank their ritual sake, bound up their heads with a silk scarf, and took their samurai swords into the planes with them to fly out and crash into the Yankee ships. Being small carriers, and stationed to the south of the main fleet off Okinawa, we were not attacked in the open sea, but every two weeks or so we had to provision with beans and bombs, literally about all we took aboard, at a little island, Kerama-retto, a supply base near Okinawa. The place had a bad feel. The entrance to what was the flooded center of an old volcano was a long, narrow passage in which there was no room to maneuver. The passage was deep but the sides so narrow that you could nearly reach out and touch the brown rock as the ship slid slowly through. In this situation you were a sitting duck for any kamikaze that came along, and on May 1 one of them took the entire flight deck off our sister ship, the USS *Sangamon,* as she was leaving Kerama-retto. We went there as infrequently as possible and were able to fight off attacks, never getting hit.

May 7: Germany surrendered, and the hope of an end to the war became more real. But there was still the fear of the landings on the Japanese homeland. I can barely remember now what it was like to be always a bit afraid, never to escape that slight sinking feeling in the gut, to awake wet with sweat at night in that unbelievably crowded compartment and hear men here and there crying out in nightmares.

Eventually it came to an end. The battle was won at Okinawa, and land-based planes began to take over the bombing of Ishigaki and Miyako. On June 17 we left for the Philippines and the island of Leyte after eighty-five days at sea, one of the longest cruises of the war, and recognized, with other exploits, by a Presidential Unit Citation for the *Suwanee,* and Distinguished Flying Crosses and Air Medals for the flyers. The Philippines had been retaken but there was little to do in Leyte except walk around in the mud of the marketplace and try to decide whether the cane whiskey the Filipinos sold under names like Freddie Walker, Red and Black, and Three Stooges would blind you as surely as was rumored. We decided it would and returned to the ship muddy but sober.

TWELVE

Peace

By June 26, 1945, we were off to Balikpapan to cover the Australian landings on Borneo. Borneo had been a source of Japanese oil since the first days of the war, and at one time, so pure was the product, they were burning it in naval boilers without refining it. That was dangerous, though, and at the Battle of the Philippine Sea one of their new carriers, hit by a submarine torpedo, blew up instantly, so volatile was the unrefined Borneo oil. It still was exciting, passing Celebes and going down through the Makassar Strait, taking us back to those first days of the war when the Australian, Dutch, and American fleets had been overwhelmed off Indonesia. Now there were no Japanese to be found anywhere, not a plane in the air to defend the refineries, and we flew back and forth without dropping our bombs, since the Australians were going ashore without opposition. It was my last combat mission, if it can be called that, but I did not know it at the time.

July 7, back to Leyte, where we anchored and took the planes ashore for several weeks on one of those remarkable coral landing strips the Seabees built across the Pacific. The strips were a beautiful hard white, made of living coral dredged up from the nearby bay and kept alive by being watered daily with seawater from a sprinkler truck. As long as it was watered it continued to live, and every day the steamrollers crushed it smooth and hard again. A dazzling light bounced up from that white surface and gave terrible sunburns to the unwary.

One day we flew to Manila, a hundred miles or so to the north, to pick up mail. The flight led across the jungles of Samar where, flying a few hundred feet off the ground, we saw back in the forests high waterfalls and huge flowers, ten or fifteen feet across, and small villages at the end of long dirt trails. Dyer had business, so Mullins and I hitched a ride into Manila, which was all ruins. One concrete building alone stood by the river, painted dark green and offering Red Cross doughnuts, but everywhere else was deep in mud and sour with the smell of broken timber and crumbled mortar.

The war was clearly winding down, and for the moment the whole vast army and navy that had come to the western Pacific waited for reinforcement from Europe and gathered strength for the fall landings on the southernmost Japanese island, Kyushu. August 3, we went from Leyte to Okinawa, arriving on the 6th and anchoring in the middle of the great fleet assembled there. We flew off the field at Naha from time to time, picking up mail, but mostly we sat at anchor, played bridge, and listened to rumors: that the war was about to end; that Japan would surrender; that the B-29 Superfortresses based on the Marianas were burning entire islands flat; that there was some new secret weapon!

Sometimes we would be organized into baseball teams and sent to a small nearby island to play softball against teams from other ships. The worst players were assigned to the weed-covered outfield, where poisonous snakes sometimes lay concealed, which made for the most cautious outfielders in the world. Any fly ball to the outfield was good for at least a hit, and usually a home run. One day a fielder stumbled over an unexploded five-inch shell and, shouting for us to look, held it in the air and then dropped it into a well, where it exploded with a loud bang. When the dust cleared, the outfielder was standing there looking dazed, blood pouring out of his nose and ears from the concussion.

Returning from our baseball game, we came alongside the ship and began to send sailors up the gangway. At that moment another landing craft came up carrying officers, including the executive officer of the *Suwanee*—a small, dark, mean man—who stood up in the bow, dead drunk, shouting in a loud voice to the officer-of-the-deck, "Get those fucking enlisted men out of there and get us aboard." Protocol was that officers always take precedence in landing, and our boat shoved off immediately, circling while the officers staggered up the gangway after their afternoon of drinking in the officers' club. The gap between enlisted men and officers in the American navy during World War II was medieval. Enlisted men accepted the division as a necessary part of military life, but it never occurred to us that it in any way diminished our status as freeborn citizens who, because of a run of bad luck and some unfortunate circumstances like the Depression, just happened to be down for a brief time. "When we get rich" were still words deep in everybody's psyche. But the exec's words, "those fucking enlisted men," spoke of deep and permanent divisions. He obviously really disliked us, and his words made shockingly clear that he, and maybe the other officers he represented, had no sense that we had shared great dangers and won great victories together. Apparently the exec was not very popular elsewhere, for the captain confined him to quarters for a failure of discipline not long after.

"August 13—they tell us that the war has ended—*Pennsylvania* was torpedoed near us tonight." So reads a note near the end of my flight log. The word crept around the ship during the late afternoon and evening, half-believed, half-not. We had heard several days before that two bombs of a new type had been dropped on Japan, causing tremendous damage. But we agreed after much discussion that bombs were only bombs, no matter how much devastation they caused, and that the Japanese were a tough people, the toughest we had ever seen. It was concluded unlikely that they would surrender, and so the landings were still ahead. Surrender rumors persisted, however, and eventually the captain came on the loudspeaker to tell us that there was a truce, and that the end of the war was likely. There was nothing to do to celebrate, and I felt nothing, absolutely nothing—no exhilaration, no triumph, no anticipation of going home, not even the simple pleasure of having survived. At best there was some symmetry. Having begun the war at Pearl Harbor nearly four years earlier, the wheel had now come full circle, and I was ending it on the last battlefield.

By now it was dark, and around us on ships where the discipline must have been light men began firing guns in the air, creating a sky full of tracers and explosives. It seemed irritating rather than celebratory, an unseemly response somehow to so long and difficult a struggle, an anticlimax in which the end did not live up either to expectations or to what had gone before.

We made our way up the Japanese coast, stopping at one small port after another, where, to our surprise, the people were quite friendly and seemed to bear us no grudge whatsoever. We felt the same way about them. September 15, the last entry in my flight log, records a flight of three and a half hours picking up mail from Okinawa and taking it to the ship. I knew it was most likely my last flight and patted the deck fondly when we landed.

September 17, anchored in Nagasaki, where the second atomic bomb had exploded. A long deep inlet to the town that straggled up the valley and the nearby hill. Aircraft carriers have a lot of space on the hangar deck when all the planes are parked on the flight deck, and we were there to provide transport for thousands of Allied prisoners who were working in the mines at the head of the valley. Many of them had been there since the fall of the Dutch empire and the surrender of Singapore. In the end they did not come aboard but went to hospital ships that followed us into the harbor. In the stone customhouse I picked up some Japanese forms and looked out the door at the devastation of the houses and the factories, among which people—in the Asian way wearing surgical masks, like magical protectors from harm—were wandering aimlessly up and down among the rubble, looking for what had once been there. Back on the deck of the ship we stood and watched the people going back and forth all day long. The site was fascinating but not particularly terrible to see. It looked like any other bombed-out town, and there was no way of comprehending that one bomb had done it all in an instant. We knew nothing of U-235, nor of the technology involved, and we cared almost nothing for the morality of using the bomb, the question that has so occupied generations since. The issue may have been raised but only to be disposed of quickly. They had attacked us, we had finished them with whatever means was at hand. That is what war is.

Each of us felt, further, that those two bombs had saved our lives—not life in general, but our own felt, breathing life. No one who was not there will ever understand how fatalistically we viewed the invasion of Japan. It had to be done, and would be, but each of us felt that survival was unlikely. Our ship was scheduled to provide close inshore support for the troops landing on the beaches. The Japanese would kamikaze us with every plane, small and large, that they had left. The fighting ashore would be ferocious, and if shot down, which was likely on frequent close-support missions, we would have little chance of escape. I had, I felt, lived through a lot, miraculously without a scratch, but my good luck could not continue on into still another year of war. I was now twenty-two, and years had been spent in a great war, mostly at sea in combat conditions. I was not, I realized, ever going to get a chance to live out my late teens and early twenties in the normal way. I wasn't sentimental about it. After all, my whole generation had spent those years in the service, and it was the great adventure of our time; but I did want what was left of life. The bomb gave it to me, and while others do feel otherwise, I remain grateful and unashamed. In after years, when I was on the faculty of liberal universities where it was an unquestioned article of faith that dropping the bombs was a crime against humanity and another instance of American racism,

I had to bite my tongue to keep silent, for to have said how grateful I was to the bomb would have marked me as a fascist—the kind I had spent five years fighting!

A few days later we worked our way up the eastern coast of Honshu to the great bay of Tokyo, Mount Fuji visible in the background, and anchored at the Japanese naval base of Yokosuka. There was grim satisfaction in being there, for all around us were the rusty hulls and twisted upper decks of battleships and cruisers that had been sunk at their moorings by naval attacks from our carriers at the end of the war. Ashore, everything as far as the eye could see had been leveled by the fire raids of the B-29 Superfortresses. Here and there a single cement or steel-framed building still stood, only making the rest of the devastation seem more vast and empty. Going ashore one gray day in November, I walked around the abandoned machine shops of the naval base. There were small ships, half-finished, on the way: a midget submarine here, a subchaser there. Inside the sheds the lathes and mechanical hammers stretched out into the gloom. Like most Americans, I had never understood how the Japanese had had the daring to attack a nation so much larger and more powerful than Nippon, and here in this grim place, with ruin all around, the folly of their original attack was manifest.

Despite my age, my promotion to chief petty officer was due, and I decided, since I would be leaving the service shortly, to push for it before discharge. The personnel officer grumbled about the paperwork; he may still have been thinking of that lost day reporting to Livermore. I think too that he thought I looked much too young for the senior enlisted rating in the navy, but regulations required that my case at least be considered, and in due time I was made aviation chief ordnanceman, acting appointment, temporary—about as many qualifications as you can get—which meant that I could hold on to the rating after a year only by signing up for another four years. With flight pay I now earned nearly two hundred dollars a month, which seemed to me like riches, enough to tempt me for a brief time to sign on again and do my twenty before retiring on a pension. I bought some gray trousers and gray shirts and an overseas cap with a chief's insignia in the ship's store of a big nearby tender, and I moved up to the chiefs' quarters. Lots of room, real mattresses, special chow, and a mess room in which to sit and read, listen to the radio, or talk.

There wasn't much talk since most of the old chiefs had already found transport on some ship going home. Release from service was by an elaborate point system built on the number of years of service, size of family, time overseas, decorations, and so on. I had a very high number—more than anyone else in the squadron—but the squadron commander refused to release me on the grounds that I had skills that were still needed. This was foolish, for we didn't even have planes anymore, but he was trying to keep some kind of an organization together, and I was part of his scheme, just as I had been long ago on the beach in New Caledonia. I complained, bitterly, daily, and was finally told that I could go in late November, but on a group of old battleships that were about to depart on an around-the-world voyage—Hong Kong, Singapore, Bombay, Suez, Gibraltar, and Norfolk. I should have leaped at the chance to be a passenger on such a splendid cruise, but I could only think of getting home, and the three months of the trip seemed much too long. So I stayed, waiting in the nearly empty chiefs' quarters for a more direct ship home. A typhoon blew through the bay, and I sat alone in a chair and slid back and forth across the steel deck of the mess room as the ship rolled thirty or more degrees. Not another soul was about.

Then the *Suwanee* got orders to take passengers aboard (they would sleep on cots on the hangar deck) and proceed by way of Pearl Harbor to San Diego to release her crew and be decommissioned. I had decided against making a career of the navy, wanting to go instead to the University of Wyoming. But I had not saved a penny during my years in service. I had alloted my stepfather maybe a thousand dollars from my pay. He eventually returned it all, scrupulously paying interest, when he sold our old ranch, but I had no idea at the time that he would or could ever repay me. Like Jack, the proverbial sailor, I had gambled, drunk, and partied away all my pay—"Jack's a cinch, and every inch a sailor"—and now I was going home nearly broke, with no salable skill. Who needed an aerial gunner? But the government had, in its wisdom, passed the G.I. Bill so that I was miraculously saved from my own folly and guaranteed tuition money for any college I could get into, plus sixty-five dollars a month to live on. I heard later that the G.I. Bill was actually passed to prevent twelve million veterans from flooding the job market, but whatever the reason, it was a gift not to be looked in the mouth, and its unanticipated effects proved as far-reaching for the country as the Homestead Act or the transcontinental railroad.

Upon promotion every chief petty officer was given a clothing allowance of three hundred dollars to buy new uniforms. I had drawn my allowance and had saved the dough to get home and live on. Since I was leaving the navy, no need to buy chief's dress uniforms. But three hundred was nothing; I would spend it in a couple of months buying beer and hamburgers. Better to risk everything.

We had been running a poker game in the squadron compartment for some time, into which all my recent pay had gone. I hesitated, but why not? You had to show a hundred dollars to get a seat, so I sat down and put my hundred in front of me. The game was desultory and low level for a time, and some of the familiar players from the squadron began to drop out. Then, drawn by the game, some hard-eyed gamblers from among our passengers began to drift in—hairy, strangely clothed, armed with knives, hatchets, and other weapons.

The game began to pick up pace a bit. I won a few hands at first, nothing much, but enough to permit me to keep on playing on other people's money. Once the outsiders came in it became the kind of game where you had always to protect yourself. Any sign of weakness and they would use big rolls of bills to force you to throw down a winning hand by running the betting so high that you would drop out. Money was the weapon, and if you were nervous and defensive, worried about losing what you had, you were done for in a short time. So long as you were playing with winnings, however, you could, without being reckless, see bets, even outsized ones, when you knew you had a reasonable chance of winning.

Operating in this way, I began to win steadily. Nothing big in the way of hands. Losing often, but winning just a bit more than I lost. Full houses and fours of a kind were not seen very often in the game that night. A pair of sixes would win a big pot over a pair of fours. Sometimes even a king-high hand would win over a jack-high one. The thing was to stay when it felt right and get out early when it was obvious you had little chance. The evening went on into morning, and the people who wanted to sleep where we were playing, sitting on bunks around a few wooden ammunition boxes with a blanket for cover, went off to find empty bunks elsewhere. But for the most part the watchers were as intense as the players. It was that kind of game. Tense and hostile. There was one other player from the squadron left in the game besides me. A pale, red-headed southerner, he whined a lot about losing the money he had won from us over the past several months to buy a little home for his little family. That money had been stored up in a big roll of pale green U.S. postal money orders, bought at the ship's post office—our only way of stashing money—and now as he lost steadily, the money orders came out, one by one, a hundred dollars at a time, and were endorsed, each one a railing gone from his future porch, a window here, a door there. He couldn't quit until it was all gone, early in the morning, and I suppose I should have felt sorry for him, but all his sanctimony about his family and home built on my money, among others', made each extracted money order pure delight.

By daybreak I knew that I had won a good bit of money, but it is considered a sign of weakness to count your money during a game, showing either fear or greed, probably both. So I just kept stuffing the money in my pocket, changing little bills for big ones when the pot needed change, plugging along. Somewhere in the early morning I began to realize that the gods had once again been very good to me, and that rather than emerging from the navy broke, I was likely, with a little sense, to come out with enough money to make college more than possible.

Winners who leave games like this one abruptly are heartily disliked, and there can be trouble in a game this big. Preparation for departure has to be carefully built up, and so about ten in the morning I began to yawn ostentatiously, talk about work that had to be done that day, and then to say that I could only play six more hands, maybe seven, but no more than eight. This was thought fair since, with warning, the losers— and there were some big ones—were given at least a chance to win back their money. It was all ritual, gambler's manners, but it was important, and to make leaving easier I lost some money in the last hands, quite a lot, unnecessarily. I didn't throw in good hands, but I bet weak ones harder than I ought.

Then, about noon, having used up all my chips so that I didn't have to linger cashing in, I got up, said so long and got the hell out of there. In a deserted corner outside I stopped to count my money. Over three thousand dollars, far more than I had ever had before. Hard to realize now what a fortune it was then. I had played the fool often enough before to know that I had to do something, so I went up to the post office, paid for thirty $100 money orders made out to my stepfather, put them in several envelopes addressed to him, and dropped them down the mail slot. I still had several hundred dollars to live on until I got home, and as the ship got under way for Pearl Harbor and San Diego, I got into my new bunk in the chiefs' quarters, where the bunks were always down—in fact, they couldn't be raised—and slept the dreamless sleep of the fortunate. Good luck substitutes for other virtues!

Pearl Harbor was greatly changed. Liquor, not just beer, was for sale in the bars and by the bottle. The lights were on all over town, and liberty extended to midnight, although no one cared if you were later than that. The navy was clearly falling apart: everyone was going home, all the rules were suspended, and I only hoped the engineers would stay in the boiler room long enough to get the *Suwanee* back to the States. In one bar out near the Royal Hawaiian Hotel I got to drinking with some sailors from the destroyer *Hughes*, which had taken me off the *Hornet* at the Battle of Santa Cruz more than three years before. They all remembered it well, as did I, and I insisted on buying drinks for everyone, until we all went our separate ways, for discharge and for "Uncle Sugar"—the alphabet flags designating Uncle Sam and the United States. No one seemed to be staying in the navy.

THIRTEEN

Uncle Sugar

In early December we rounded Point Loma, and I reflected on what had happened since I had sailed past it for the first time on the way to Pearl Harbor in November 1941. Now the war was over, and I was a different person. But I wasted few glances backward. All the desires pent up by the long years in service longed for the future. I was eager to get out, meet people, go to college, and begin, so I thought in my innocence, to understand things.

Returning servicemen were gathered in barracks at the head of San Diego Bay and there separated into drafts going to the discharge points nearest to where they had enlisted. Bremerton Navy Yard, opposite Seattle across the always gray and foggy Puget Sound, was where the sailors who came from Wyoming—not too many—went, and in a few days a draft of about twenty from northwestern states was assembled to go by rail to Bremerton. As the senior in the group, I was put in charge. Not an enviable job. There were some real fuck-ups in this draft. I was given tickets and cash for meals for the entire group and told to dole out only so much to each sailor at each meal. Fighting with them about how much money they should get at a time was too much of a problem, and I had had enough of enforcing discipline on people much older and rougher than myself, so I gave each of them their full meal money at one time. The result was predictable. They drank it up at once, and after they sobered up began complaining about being hungry, which impressed me not at all.

In the effort to get millions of servicemen back to their homes, every piece of railway rolling stock in the country was hauled out of the yards and put in service. We were on some old and dusty cars with faded red-plush seats that had been sitting for years on some siding of the Southern Pacific Railroad and were now made up, as was, into a train. They were cold, with no diner or any other facilities. You had to jump off at the frequent stops, rush into a diner, take whatever was available, and run back to the train, which would then sit there for another few hours. But no one wanted to risk missing the train.

It wasn't too bad until the second day, when it became obvious that the car was infested with fleas—incredibly hungry, beady, black fleas. I might have endured the bites except that I had taken my shoes off to sleep and been bitten all over the soles of my feet. The itching was unbearable, and as we jerked our way, stop and go, through Sacramento, I spotted down a dark street the neon sign of a drugstore, still open late at night. I didn't want to chance missing the train, but the itch was maddening, so, barefoot, I set off running down the street, burst into the drugstore, shouted "something for fleabites," paid for the ointment, and raced back down the street just in time to catch the last car of the train as it was pulling out.

It took three long nights and days to make our way up through California and Oregon to northern Washington, but we made it at last into Seattle and took the ferry across to Bremerton and the separation center. A physical examination, clearance of all pay due us, a check for the three hundred dollars separation money, a golden lapel button known as a ruptured duck to show that you had been honorably discharged, and then the discharge itself. And so after four years, eight months, and seventeen days I walked out, my own man again, free to determine how I would spend my time and my life.

Exactly what to do with this freedom, however, was not obvious. So I took only a few tentative steps. After buying and changing into a civilian jacket and some ill-fitting pants, anxious to get out of uniform, I took the bus to Salem, Oregon, where Ruth was still teaching school. She and I had corresponded without much feeling off and on over the last year, and I felt that I ought to see her again; perhaps we ought to get married. That, after all, was what everyone else did. She was pretty and excited to see me, but I realized right away that there was no feeling of love on my side. After a strained night together I protested that I had to get back to Wyoming, picked up my bag, and walked a long walk with her down to the bus station. I felt cruel but determined not to tie myself down at the beginning of my freedom. She was understandably bitter, and, muttering that someone as cold as I was would have no trouble making his way in the world, she turned her back on the bus and walked away. I went to Wyoming to cash my money orders, buy an old car, drive out to California to see the Boones, and with Dick, now discharged also, set off across country to New York, to see what the future held.

The law seemed the right kind of profession for me, but in my studies at Williams College, where I went after one term at Columbia, I found myself more and more attracted to the kind of literature—Shakespeare's *Hamlet* and Dostoyevsky's *Brothers Karamazov*—that portrayed life in all its fullness, intensity, and immediacy. Other subjects that commanded more of the interest, and the rewards, of the world—biology, economics, political science—seemed too abstract and distant from the experience of being human. Williams gave me a fellowship to go to England to study at Oxford for two years, and afterward I went to graduate school at Yale. By the time I had my doctorate in English literature I was thirty years old and had a wife and two (later four) children. Good fortune gave me a job and in time a chair at Yale, where for twenty years I taught and wrote books on the Renaissance and satire. My special study was the plays of William Shakespeare, which for me were "wisdom literature," a complete world in themselves, like the Bible, that made sense of the actual world.

In the late sixties and early seventies I was the associate and then the acting provost at Yale and during those contentious times in the university administration found that all battles are not fought in declared wars.

In 1973 I moved from Yale to Princeton, a greater move than it might seem on the map, to become dean of the Graduate School. After a term at that strenuous job I returned to teaching, research, and writing until I retired from Princeton in 1988, at the age of sixty-five. Retirement gave me an opportunity to write the present book, and, until 2000 and full retirement, to direct a national graduate fellowship program in the humanities for the Andrew W. Mellon Foundation.

In our time veterans of later wars have complained that they were not welcomed when they came home. No parades, no recognition of what they had done by those for whom they had supposedly done it. I think this must be the feeling of all veterans from Caesar's legions to the present. The end of wars is anticlimactic; no one knows what to do or what to say. And once they are over almost everyone used to be willing to forget them. For myself, I never wasted a moment worrying that no one really seemed to know that I had been gone for five years, and the ones who did soon tired of talking about it, very soon. But who cares? What matters is to have survived, to have escaped from the many traps death and war set for us.

INDEX